ISBN 3-88053-017-3

JEWS IN GERMANY
UNDER PRUSSIAN RULE

An exhibition by the
Bildarchiv
Preussischer Kulturbesitz, Berlin,
in co-operation with the
Leo Baeck Institute, New York

Conceived and edited by Roland Klemig,
Director of the Bildarchiv
Preussischer Kulturbesitz, Berlin

Assistant Editor
Eva-Maria Klemig, Berlin

Art Directors
Max Ley, Konrad Zwingmann, Berlin

Photo Reproductions
Dietmar Katz, Berlin
Knud Petersen, Berlin
Fritz-Walter Wollner, Berlin

Design and Production
L+Z Grafik-Design, Berlin
AS-Fotosatz, Angela Schulze, Berlin

Printing
Alphabet KG, Berlin

Equipment
Heimann & Co KG, Berlin

Translations
Gabrielle Bamberger, New York, N.Y.
Sybille Grimme, Cambridge, England
Paul F. Guenther, Edwardsville, Ill.
Walter F. Peterson, Berlin
Peter Th. Walther, Berlin

Advisers
Alex Bein, Jerusalem
Ulrich Dunker, Berlin
Rachel Freudenthal, Berlin
Walter Grab, Tel Aviv
Fred Grubel, New York, N.Y.
Michael Heymann, Jerusalem
Reinhard Ruerup, Berlin

Published and distributed by Bildarchiv
Preussischer Kulturbesitz,
Hallesches Ufer 76, 1000 Berlin 61

We would like to thank all those
who generously gave of their
time to advise us on this project.
Their contributions, both large
and small, have been invaluable.

The exhibition in the United States
is made possible by help of the
Auswaertiges Amt (Foreign Office)
of the Federal Republic of Germany
and by generous support of
Lufthansa German Airlines.

JEWS IN GERMANY

UNDER PRUSSIAN RULE

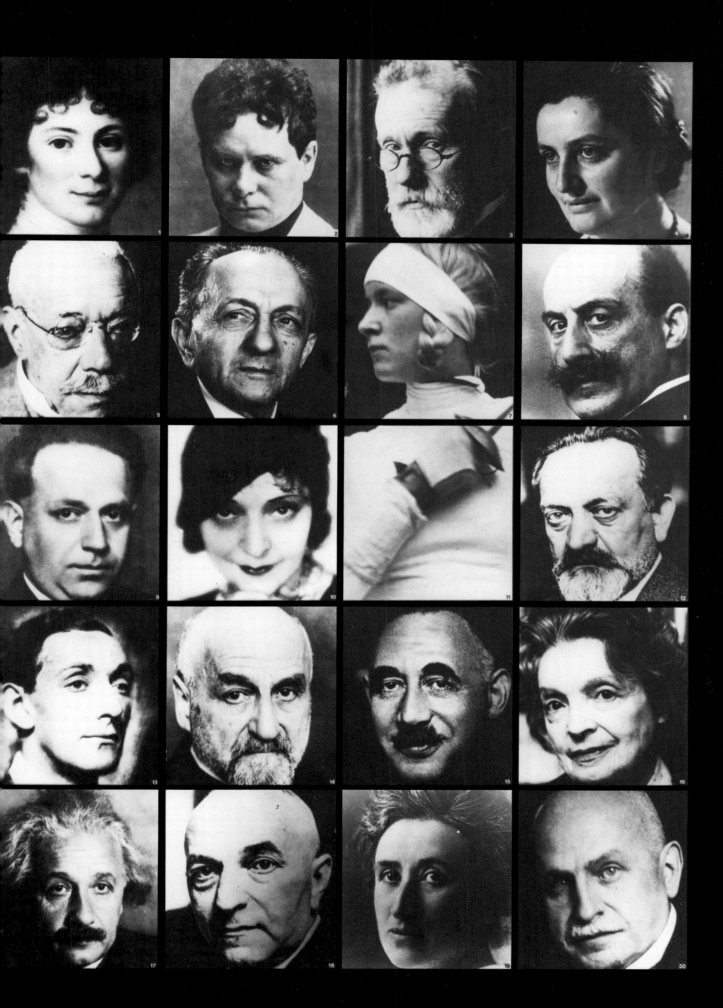

1 Sara Loewen (1769-1839), feminist
2 Maximilian Harden (1861-1927),
  author and publisher
3 Paul Ehrlich (1854-1915),
  bacteriologist and chemist
4 Hannah Karminski (1897-1942),
  social worker
5 James Simon (1851-1932),
  merchant and philanthropist
6 Eugen Bandmann (1874-1948),
  lawyer and politician
7/11 Helene Mayer (1910-1953),
  sportswoman, fencer
8 Max Liebermann (1847-1935),
  impressionist painter
9 Kurt Tucholsky (1890-1935),
  author and political satirist
10 Fritzi Massary (1882-1969), actress
12 Emil Orlik (1870-1932), painter
13 Paul Graetz (1890-1938), actor
14 Ignatz Jastrow (1856-1937),
  economist
15 Ernst Heilmann (1881-1940),
  politician
16 Nelly Sachs (1891-1970), poetess
17 Albert Einstein (1879-1955), physicist
18 Julius Moses (1868-1942),
  physician and politician
19 Rosa Luxemburg (1871-1919),
  politician
20 Leo Wolff (1870-1958), lawyer

Preface

Our exhibition begins with the destruction of the Temple in Jerusalem in 70 C.E., an event which led to the dispersion of the Jewish people, the diaspora. We present this prehistory to emphasize the fact that the history of the Jews in the diaspora is tied to the history of the nations in which they lived. Hence, the subject "Jews in Germany" is a chapter of German history.

The history of the "Jews in Germany," however, is not only a German problem but also one shared by the Christian Occident. Our exhibition draws attention to the first pogroms carried out under the sign of the cross.

The Crusades initiated a new period for the Jews: the systematic deprivation of their rights and their degradation. A derogatory image of the Jews, in part moulded and reinforced by Christian dogma — became ingrained in the hearts and minds of men. The Protestant Reformation of the 16th century hardly improved either the lot or image of the Jews.

It was not until the beginning of the 19th century that Jews gradually gained legal acceptance. At the same time social forces were developing which were to have fateful consequences for Jews and non-Jews in the 20th century. Napoleon's victory over the Prussian state in 1812 was the catalyst for social, economic, and judicial reforms. As a result of these reforms, Jews were recognized as citizens. The reactionary measures instituted at the Congress of Vienna (1815) repudiated many of the liberal reforms. And in the wake of pseudo-scientific theories, medieval "anti-Judaism" was replaced by racism and "anti-Semitism."

Equality of rights for Jews, firmly established in 1869 by the North German Federation, and apparently realized in the Weimar Republic (1918-1933), proved to be little more than an illusion for the majority of Jews. As business partners, intellectuals, and artists, they were rarely admitted into the social circles of their non-Jewish countrymen.

The consequences of the anti-Jewish components of Nazi barbarism were an unforeseen, unimaginable yet logical conclusion to centuries of intolerance, injustice, and hatred. It marked the end of a marriage based on circumstances ... a marriage which from the beginning was devoid of all love. Mass murder was the end of this relationship. And the end of German Jewry also marked the end of the German Reich.

Originally called "Juden in Preussen" (Jews in Prussia), this exhibition opened in September 1981 in Berlin. Thereafter, it appeared in various cities in the Federal Republic of Germany. The catalogue for the German exhibition is published by Harenberg Kommunikation in Dortmund; its fourth edition was printed in the summer of 1983.

The press responded to the exhibition in both factual and emotional terms. The *Jerusalem Post* regarded it as "a dramatic barometer of history ... one of the most interesting exhibitions relating to Jews ...." For those who visit this exhibition, the *Berliner Wirtschaft* asserted, it will become evident that it presents "a chapter of German cultural and intellectual history .... An exhibition of this scope," the writer concluded, "has not yet been presented in such depth and with such honesty in Germany." Most reviewers and visitors agreed with the commentator from *Sender Freies Berlin* when she observed: "What we need is information on the history of Jews in Germany."

The exhibition, however, not only lists facts from the past, but also presents a history to be remembered for the future. "The most frightening aspect," remarked Ernst Benda, the former Chief Justice of the German Constitutional Court, "is the fact that we do not know whether it can once again be repeated somewhere, sometime."
"Even if it causes us great pain," commented a political official from Westphalia, "we must also live with this chapter of our past and learn from it."

All are answerable for the deeds committed in our names, this is true not only for today but also for tomorrow. Thus, the systematic propagation of stereotypes by politicians and journalists has to be combatted. "Love thy neighbour as thyself" refers not only to your next of kin or friend but also to the stranger who enters your house and to those whose beliefs and ideas you might not share or might not even know. The basis of our freedom should be the liberty of the nonconformist, wrote Johann Jacoby, a member of the 1848 Prussian National Assembly.

This postulate should be ever present in our minds; and we should be especially aware of it before we judge or pass judgements on others.

Roland Klemig
Berlin, January 1984

A Book Is Their Fatherland

With the destruction of the province of Judea in 70 C.E., the Jewish people ceased to exist as a nation. The seven-branched candelabra from the destroyed Jerusalem Temple was displayed in the triumphal procession of the conqueror (2).

At Massada, the fortress-palace which Herod had built at the western shore of the Dead Sea (1), Jewish combatants continued to resist the Romans for three years after the conquest of Jerusalem. Before the fortress fell, they all committed suicide.

The Western Wall was all that remained from the destroyed Temple (3).

After their expulsion, the Jews settled in many parts of the Roman Empire. Adherence to the Bible and tradition became the bond which held them together in the Diaspora (4).

"A book is their fatherland, their property, their ruler, their fortune and their misfortune. They live within the given boundaries of that book, and here they practise their inalienable rights: they cannot be expelled nor despised; here they are strong and admirable" (Heinrich Heine).

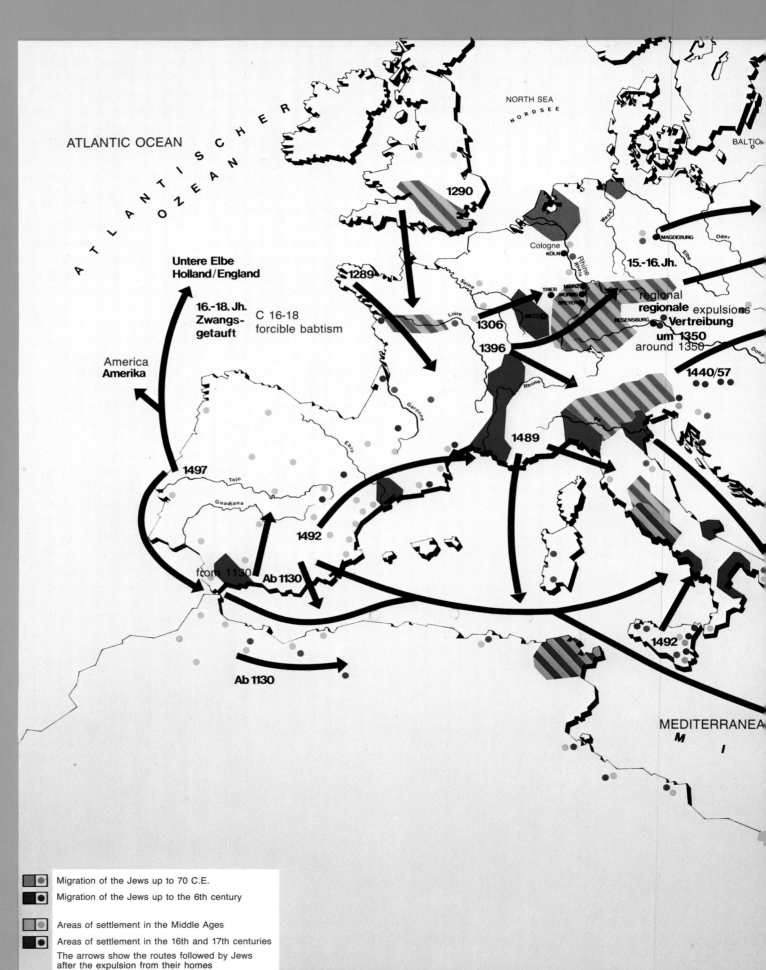

ATLANTIC OCEAN

ATLANTISCHER OZEAN

NORTH SEA
NORDSEE

BALTIC

1290

Cologne
KÖLN

Rhine
Rhein

West

Oder

MAGDEBURG

15.-16. Jh.

Untere Elbe
Holland/England

1289

Seine

Loire

TRIER MAINZ
WORMS
SPEYER

METZ

regional
regionale expulsions
Vertreibung
um 1350
around 1350

16.-18. Jh.
Zwangs-
getauft

C 16-18
forcible babtism

1306

REGENSBURG

Donau

1396

America
Amerika

Garonne

Rhone

Po

1440/57

1489

Ebro

1497

Tajo

Guadiana

1492

1492

from 1130   Ab 1130

1492

MEDITERRANEA
M   I

Ab 1130

Early History

After the destruction of Judea by the Romans in 70 C.E., the Jews dispersed and resettled in various provinces of the Roman Empire. Thus began the *Diaspora*, a life in exile. Their adherence to tradition and their faith united them. The nineteenth century Jewish poet Heinrich Heine observed that, *"A book is their fatherland, their property, their ruler, their fortune and their misfortune. They live within the given boundaries of that book, and here they practise their inalienable rights: they cannot be expelled nor despised; here they are strong and admirable."*

The Jews lived as aliens within the Christian world, and their history can only be understood in the context of a general historical background. In the agrarian society of the early Middle Ages, the Jews were primarily merchants who provided the upper class with luxury goods.

Migration of the Jews up to 70 C.E.

Migration of the Jews up to the 6th century

Areas of settlement in the Middle Ages

Areas of settlement in the 16th and 17th centuries

The arrows show the routes followed by Jews after the expulsion from their homes

... Among The People...."

(Mose V 4:27)

From the 12th century until their emancipation Jews were barred from owning land and excluded from all guilds; thus began centuries of being scorned and marked as aliens. St. Augustine (354-430), in *De Civitate Dei*, expressed the opinion that God had kept the Jews alive in the Diaspora to demonstrate the triumph of Christendom over Jewry. The church continually demanded the exclusion of the Jews from social and legal activities. Pope Innocent III singled them out in a resolution of the Fourth Lateran Council in 1215, declaring: *"... that Jews of both sexes in every Christian country and at all times must identify themselves in public by their garb, as Moses prescribed."* According to such edicts, Jews were not allowed to accept any civic posts; therefore, they were primarily engaged in trade and money lending, a business closed to Christians.

The Crusades (1096-1270) marked the beginning of pogroms for the Jews. As they journeyed to Jerusalem, the Crusaders committed massacres, primarily in the cities along the Rhine, such as Worms, Speyer, and Mainz. Synagogues were destroyed and the homes of Jews were looted. Baptism was forced upon them; they were abused and killed.

After these persecutions the plague broke out (1348-1350). The Jews were accused of having poisoned the wells from which the Christians obtained their water. Those Jews who survived the plague and persecution fled to the East and settled mainly in Poland, where they were granted liberty and unrestricted freedom to trade.

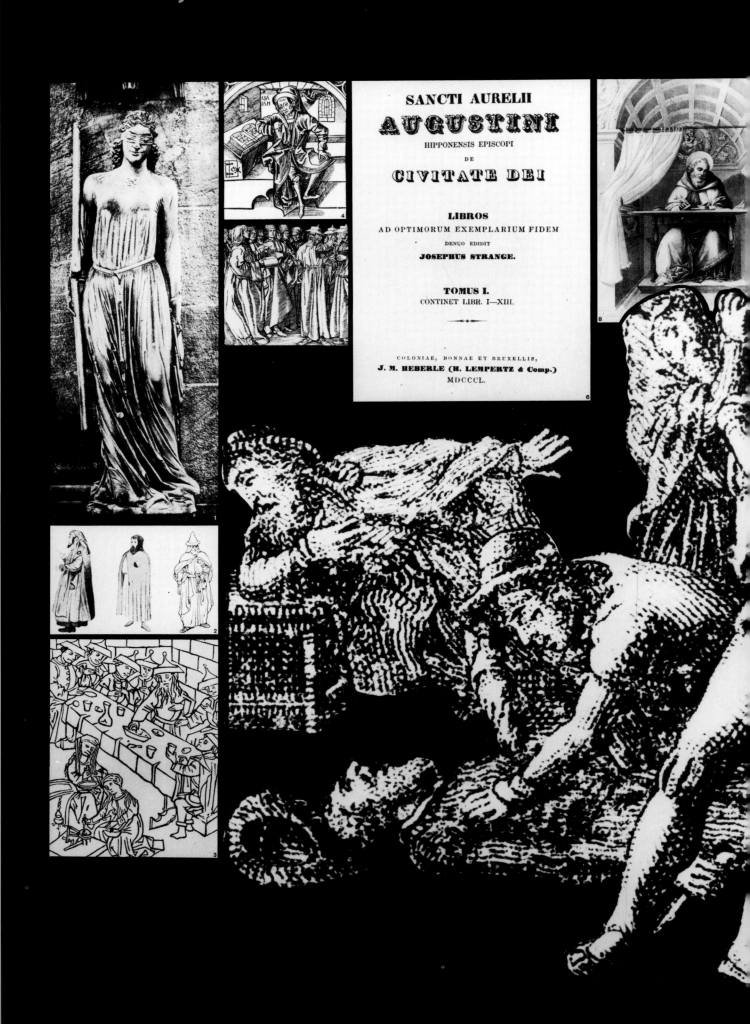

Persecution of the Jews began in Europe with the first Crusade in 1096. The Jews of Speyer, Mainz, Worms and other cities particularly suffered. The fanatic crusaders killed Jewish families, ransacked their homes, and destroyed all synagogues.

"And deep darkness engulfed us." (Samuel Ben-Jehuda, 1096).

The majority of the Jews of Worms preferred to commit suicide (15).

In the 13th century, the legal status of Jews was codified in the "Schwaben-spiegel" (13) and "Sachsenspiegel" (14).

As a young man, Luther (9) had defended the Jews in his 1523 pamphlet "That Jesus Christ was born a Jew." In his later years, Luther (11) attacked them because they did not convert. And in 1543 he declared "that they are poisonous, bitter, thieving, malicious snakes, assassins, and children of the devil... that one should put their synagogues and schools to the torch and cover that which will not burn with earth..." (10).

The Church And The Jews

According to the teachings of St. Augustine (8), as stated in his treatise "De Civitate Dei" (6), God preserved the Jews and scattered them among the peoples of the earth in order to give testimony to the triumph of Christianity over Judaism.

Pope Innocent III continued the policy toward Jews initiated by his predecessors. The Fourth Lateran Council in 1215 branded the Jews as outcasts of society.

1　The "Synagoga" at the Bamberg Cathedral
2　The round patch and the pointed hat: dress regulations for Jews in the Middle Ages
3　Jews around the table wearing pointed hats
4　Jewish scholar
5　Debate between Christian (left) and Jewish scholars
6　The "Ecclesia" at the Bamberg Cathedral

Jews in the Mark Brandenburg

The first reference to Jews in the Mark Brandenburg region is found in a document from 975; it is not until 1295 that they are mentioned as residing in Berlin. In contrast to other parts of Germany, the Jews were not legal subjects of the Emperor but of the Margrave to whom they payed their taxes. The first and oldest statute pertaining to Jews in the Mark Brandenburg was issued in Stendal in 1297. Depending upon their wealth, Jews were granted the right to settle in the town. Nonetheless, persecution continued. Elector Frederick II confiscated their assets and expelled them from his territory in 1446. Shortly thereafter the Jews were readmitted; the high tax revenues extracted from them were needed to improve the finances of Brandenburg. Moreover, Jews were needed as tradesmen, money-changers, money-lenders, and pawnbrokers. When Christians temporarily became moneylenders, most citizens in 1480 felt that *the pressure from Christian moneylenders was much greater than that from the Jewish ones.*

Religious as well as economic reasons led to the persecution of Jews. The trials of the so-called *desecration of the holy wafer* in Berlin at the beginning of the 16th century exemplify this pattern. In 1510 a Christian tinker had stolen two holy wafers and a gilded monstrance from the village church of Knobloch in the Havelland. The clergy exploited the incident and accused the Jews of the crime.

The tinker testified under torture that he had given the holy wafers to the Jews. Thereafter, more than one hundred Jews were thrown into jail. Some of them *confessed* under torture that they had murdered many Christian children in the years before. On July 19, 1510, thirty-nine Jews were sentenced to death and burned at the stake at the New Market in Berlin. After their execution, all remaining Jews were expelled from the Mark Brandenburg. The myths of the desecration of the holy wafers and ritual child murders were still believed in the 20th century.

The intensity of religious hatred did not abate in the Age of the Reformation. Although Luther at first objected to the slander of Jews, he later attacked them because they failed to convert to Christianity. He decried them in his writings and his sermons. In his book *On the Jews and their Lies*, published in 1543, Luther repeated the old accusations of ritual murder and poisoned wells. He demanded that *their synagogues and schools be burned, ... and their right to freedom of movement be completely rescinded.* These comments by Luther, whose writings and sermons were widely distributed, kept the religious hatred alive.

Thirty years after the expulsion (1540), the Jews were again allowed to settle in Brandenburg in order to breathe new life into the Polish trade. The merchant Lippold became comptroller of the mint and financial counsellor to Elector Joachim II. When Joachim died in 1571, his successor Johann Georg ordered Lippold's arrest. He was accused of embezzlement, but a thorough examination of the books revealed no wrongdoing. Thereupon, he was accused of poisoning Joachim II and of having an affair with Joachim's mistress. Under torture Lippold confessed to everything, but when judgement was given in 1573, he withdrew his confession. Once again, he was tortured. This time, he was broken on the wheel and drawn and quartered at the New Market in Berlin. Even though Lippold's innocence was proven after the execution, and his good name was restored, all Jews had to leave Brandenburg. For a century, they were banned from town and country.

During the Thirty Years War (1618-48), two-thirds of the population of the Mark Brandenburg were killed or died from the effects of the war. The economy was destroyed. In an edict of May 21, 1671, Frederick William, the "Great Elector," admitted fifty Jewish families, recently expelled from Vienna, to settle in Berlin on the condition that each family brings 10,000 talers. The Elector needed the financial power of these rich Jews to reestablish the economy and to finance his wars.

The Edict of 1671 inaugurates a new era in the history of Prussian Jews. September 10, 1671, the day the first two *Letters of Protection* were signed, marks the beginning of the Jewish community in Berlin.

Around 1700, when there were 117 Jewish families in Berlin, only seventy possessed *Letters of Protection*. Elector Fredrrick III crowned himself King Frederick I of Prussia on January 18, 1701 in Koenigsberg. He established a *Commission for the Jews* to revise their status. Although Jews were primarily judged according to their utility, this otherwise unflattering attitude also opened the way for Jewish integration into the community.

Strong social tensions existed in the Jewish community. The Viennese Jews considered themselves the aristocracy of Prussian Jewry. Like all other Jews who had become wealthy, they looked down upon those without *Letters of Protection*, as well as on simple tradesmen and peddlers. They adapted their life style more and more to that of the Christian upper class; at the same time, their appreciation of the traditional Jewish way of life lessened. This process of adapting to society was later termed *assimilation*. Yet, in spite of all internal, as well as external tensions, the community remained the centre of Jewish life. To be a Jew meant belonging to a congregation which was the focal point of their religious, cultural, and social activities. Only in that community could Jews live, only in that fellowship with other Jews could they find their identity.

The Regulations of 1730 and 1750

The *General Regulation for Jews* of September 29, 1730, established a more stringent policy towards the Jews. It was based on the new economic policies of Frederick William I, later known as the Soldier King. While rich Jews were favoured because of their economic usefulness, the less wealthy Jews continued to suffer under restrictions.

Frederick II, later known as Frederick the Great, declared after his succession to the throne in 1740 that all religions should be tolerated and that in his state *everyone should be happy in his own fashion. The Revised General Privilege and Regulation for the Jews in the Kingdom of Prussia* of 1750, however, expresses little tolerance, or humanist spirit. When Frederick the Great, as a result of his wars, discovered that his treasury was empty, he did not hesitate to impose new and higher taxes on the Jews.

The Beginnings of the Emancipation

During the Middle Ages the alien and segregated status of the Jews was accepted by the Christian population as well as by the Jews themselves. The beginning of the modern era, however, brought a decisive reversal in the relationship between Jews and non-Jews.

The gradual centralization of state functions under absolutism and the struggle of the middle classes for civil rights and equality constituted the basis for the demand by Jews for citizenship and equality under the law. This concept of emancipation became the aim of all progressive forces. As citizens of the state, the Jews were now legally entitled to civil rights. They were, however, expected to abandon their own *"national identity"* and to integrate into their respective nations as Germans, Englishmen, Frenchmen, etc.

A New View of Judaism

Moses Mendelssohn (1729-1786), son of a Tora-scribe from Dessau, and Gotthold Ephraim Lessing (1729-1781), son of a Lutheran parson from Kamenz, were significant figures at the turning point of the relationship between Jews and Christians in Germany. Mendelssohn lived under Frederick II in circumstances which Lessing described as *disgraceful oppression.* Mendelssohn did not possess a *Letter of Protection;* he therefore lived according to the General Regulation as a *tolerated* Jew. He was allowed to stay in Berlin provided he continued to work for the silk manufacturer Bernhard, a *regularly protected Jew.* In 1780 Mendelssohn wrote: *"Here in this so-called tolerant land, I live so hemmed in, so restricted on all sides by intolerance, that for the sake of my children I must lock myself up in the silk factory all day long."* Mendelssohn, who later became co-owner of that factory, was a bookkeeper, tutor, literary critic, bible translater, and philosopher.

As an orthodox Jew, he lived in a socially separate community. He perceived the exclusion of Jews as a hostile expression of an as yet unenlightened society. He advocated the acculturation of Jews to the European way of life. He described the relationship between Jewish law and state law to his fellow Jews as follows: *"Emulate the customs and obey the laws of the country into which you have been transplanted, but always be true to the religion of your fathers...."*

Resistance and Obstacles

The demand for the emancipation of the Jews in Prussia did not find broad support among the middle class or any other strata of society. The opposition of the merchant guilds and craft guilds, which had always been strongly opposed to Jewish economic activities persisted into the 18th and early 19th centuries. The Christian merchants and the manufacturers' guilds constantly urged the expulsion of Jewish competitors and demanded, often successfully, the legal curtailment of their economic activities.

Opposition to the emancipation of the Jews was not only evident in economic matters, but also in politics and cultural life. In 1793 the philosopher Johann Gottlieb Fichte said: *"There is only one way to give the Jews civil rights and that is to cut off all Jewish heads one night and to replace them with others which contain not a single Jewish idea. To protect ourselves from them, I see no other means but to conquer their Holy Land for them and to send them all back there."*

The Salons:
Encounters in No Man's Land

With the victory of the bourgeois revolution in 1791, the emancipation of the Jews in France became a reality. In Prussia only a small sector of the population, predominantly from the upper classes, continued to support the process of acculturation. At the beginning of the 19th century, following the French model, Jews and non-Jews met in the Berlin *Salons* of Rahel Levin-Varnhagen, Henriette Herz, and Dorothea Schlegel; here they discussed literary and aesthetic topics. In these drawing rooms, they were uninhibited by religious and social ties and considered themselves as *world citizens.* But in 1811, the rival conservative intellectuals also gathered in Berlin to form the *Christian-German Round Table.* Its most famous members included Johann Gottlieb Fichte, Heinrich von Kleist, Karl von Clausewitz as well as Clemens Brentano who in this circle spoke of the Jews as *"those flies that survived the Egyptian plagues."*

The First Jews In The Mark Brandenburg

The Mark Brandenburg in 1417

The first reference to Jews in the region later known as the Mark Brandenburg dates back to the year 975. At that time, Emperor Otto II gave permission for Jews from the Magdeburg area to engage in commerce with the "heathen" Slavic inhabitants of the East.

During the great plague of 1348-1350 (2, 3), the Jews were accused of poisoning the wells which provided the water for the Christian population. Horrible pogroms took place throughout Western and Central Europe. The Jews fled eastward.

In the fourteenth century, wealthy Jews were able to obtain the right to settle in Coelln, Berlin, and Spandau.

The oldest known Jewish tombstones there (10) date back to the 13th century. They were later used in the construction of the citadel wall in Spandau (5).

The "Julius Tower" of the citadel (1) was originally named "Jews' Tower." The Margrave Ludwig had given the Spandau Tower Office to his Jewish "Servant Frizen" on September 8, 1356 in recognition of his "many loyal services."

A document dated 1312 (9) mentions Jews in Berlin.

The term "Juedenhof" (Jews' Court) was first used in the 16th century and remained in use into the 20th century (4).

In 1411 the Nuremberg Burgrave Frederick Hohenzollern (6) was appointed governor of Brandenburg (8). In 1417 Emperor Sigismund gave him the Mark Brandenburg as a hereditary fief (7).

Jews Were Needed

The Elector Frederick II (5) expelled the Jews from the Brandenburg region in 1446. They were readmitted a short time later because they were needed as money-changers, financiers, pawn-brokers, and tradesmen (1-5).

When in 1480 Christians temporarily engaged in money lending, it was said that the population "suffered more from the Christians than from the Jews."

Jews Were Burned

In 1510 a Christian tinker stole a gilded monstrance and two holy wafers from the village church in Knobloch in the Havelland. The clergy used the occasion to concoct a charge against the Jews. They wanted to force Elector Joachim I Nestor into action; he did not want to expel the Jews and had actually granted them privileges. Under torture, the thief stated that he had slit the wafers and sent pieces to a number of Jews. He also claimed that he had baked the second wafer in a pie and brought it to the Spandau Synagogue. According to Catholic teaching, the holy wafer is the body of Christ.

More than one hundred Jews were incarcerated. Under torture (3) they "confessed" to having cut up the wafers (1) and to having murdered Christian children.

Thirty-nine Jews received the death sentence and were burned at the stake at the New Market in Berlin in 1510. Two of the defendants consented to be baptized before the execution; they did not die at the stake but were granted an "easier death" by the sword.

All other Jews were expelled from Brandenburg and their possessions confiscated.

The stories about the desecration of the Hosts and of ritual murder found believers until the 20th century.

Execution Of A Court-Jew

Since Jews were active in the monetary trade, they were often commissioned to mint coins (2). The merchant Lippold (1) was head of the mint and financial adviser to Elector Joachim II (4).

Upon Joachim's sudden death in 1571, his successor, Johann Georg, ordered the immediate arrest of Lippold. Lippold was charged with theft. An examination of the books, however, did not produce any evidence of wrong-doing; thereupon he was charged with poisoning Joachim II and accused of having a love affair with Joachim's mistress, Anna Sydow (5).

Under torture he "confessed" to every-thing. When sentence was passed in 1573, he repudiated his confession; again he was tortured. While beeing driven through Berlin in a cart he was tortured with fiery tongs (6), he then was drawn and quartered at the New Market (7,3).

The Synagogue was destroyed; all Jews had to leave the region of Brandenburg and were not allowed to return to the city or the region for a century.

After Lippold's execution, his innocence became evident and his name was cleared.

A Thirty Years Religious War

During the Thirty Years War (1618-1648), the population of Brandenburg suffered grievously. Two-thirds of the inhabitants were killed in the war or died as a consequence of it.

Negative Typecasting

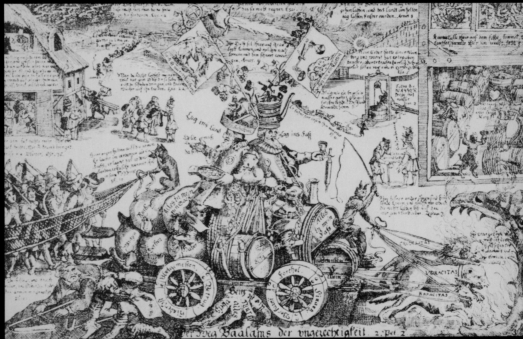

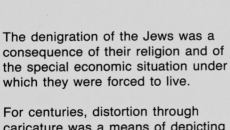

The denigration of the Jews was a consequence of their religion and of the special economic situation under which they were forced to live.

For centuries, distortion through caricature was a means of depicting them as society's outcasts (1), as children of the devil (2), as crooked dealers in grain and wine (3), as "kippers" (coinage spoilers) and corrupt money changers (4), as oppressors of Christians (5), and as subhumans (6).

Even Josel of Rosheim (1480-1554), the recognized representative of German Jewry, was defamed in a leaflet which showed him with his Talmud and money bag in front of the Golden Calf (7).

Wealthy Exiled Viennese Jews Settle In Berlin

The yearly wage for a journeyman was 38 talers and 18 silver-pennies

The yearly wage for a master mason was 77 talers and 12 silver-pennies

In order to earn 10,000 talers a journeyman would have had to work for 258 years, a master mason for 125 years

In 1675 the Great Elector Frederick William (3) defeated the Swedes in the Battle of Fehrbellin (1) with the aid of General Derfflinger (2). Four years earlier an edict (6) granted shelter to a few Jewish families exiled from Vienna (7) on the condition that each family bring at least 10,000 talers with them (8). He needed the financial power of these wealthy Jews to develop the economy and to pay for his wars.

September 10, 1671, the day the first "Letters of Protection" were issued to two Jewish families from Vienna, marks the founding of the Berlin Jewish community.

In contrast, the Huguenots who came from France 14 years later as fugitives (5) were admitted without any conditions. They were Protestants. Allegedly, Frederick William even sold his silverware (4) to facilitate their integration.

Brandenburg-Prussia under the Great Elector (until 1688)

The Elector's Capital

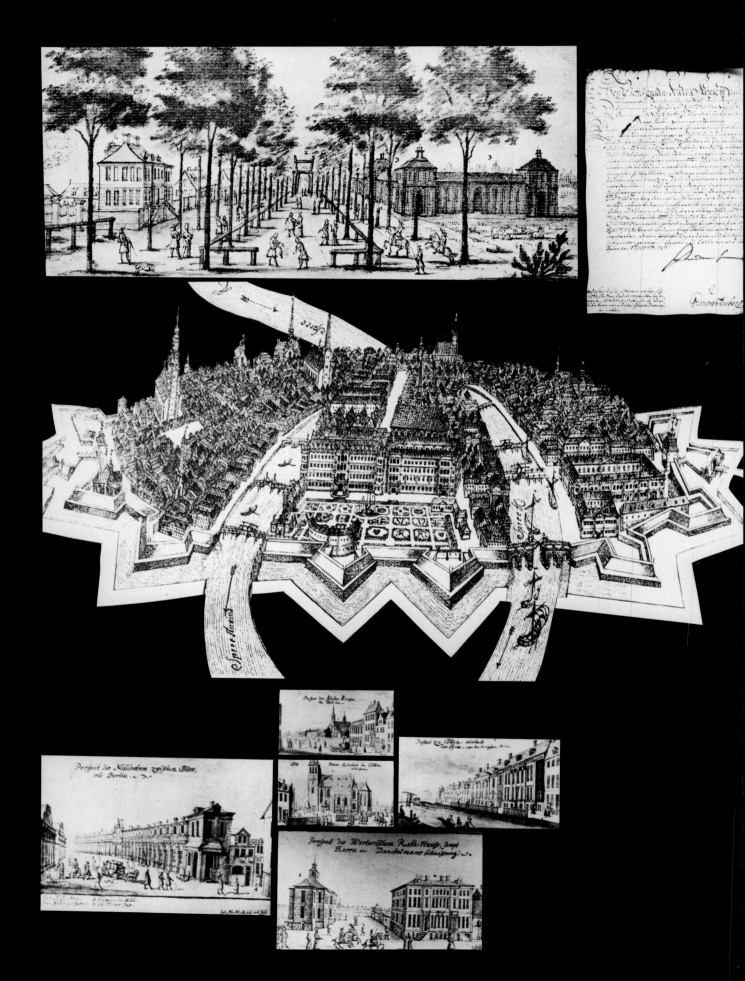

By 1700 Berlin was home for 117 Jewish families, of whom only 70 possessed "Letters of Protection."

These dealt in diverse merchandise, including gold, silver, and precious stones. This brought them into closer contact with many of their Christian fellow-citizens. Jews without "Letters of Protection," mostly peddlers and junk dealers, traded merchandise produced by Christian craftsmen outside of guild control.

The Elector Becomes King

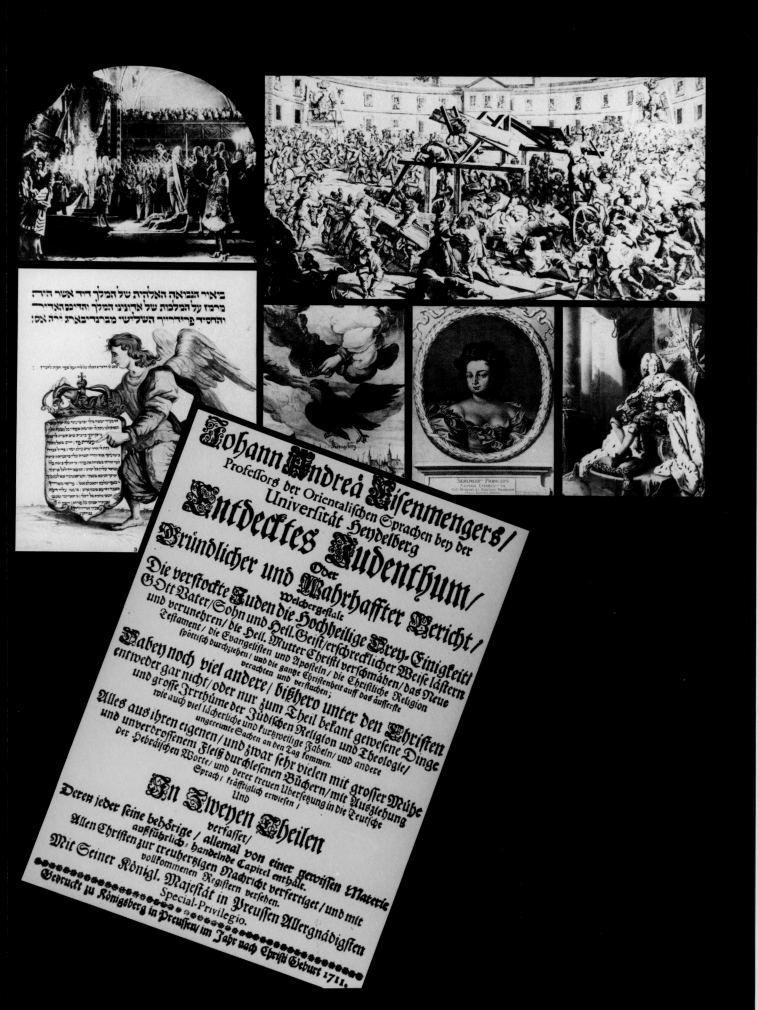

On January 18, 1701 in Koenigsberg (1), the Elector Frederick III had himself crowned Frederick I, King of Prussia (6). He then crowned Sophie Charlotte (5) as his queen. Wine flowed, an ox was roasted (2); the people honoured their king.

The "privileged" Berlin Jew Simon Wolff Brandes used the 21st Psalm to compose a homage, "A divine secret revealed" (3, Hebrew title; 4, German title), in which he asked, on behalf of the Jewish population, that the new king be granted power, splendour, and a long life.

Frederick I renewed the "Letters of Protection" for all Jews, which made further settlement possible. But he demanded 1,000 ducats per year from the Jews of Berlin in addition to a payment of 20,000 talers during his coronation year.

In 1711 he sponsored the reissue of a rabidly anti-Semitic work by the Protestant theologian Johann Andreas Eisenmenger (7). In order to avoid the imperial ban on the distribution of this book, it was printed in Koenigsberg, a city beyond the jurisdiction of the emperor.

The Beginnings Of The Berlin Jewish Community

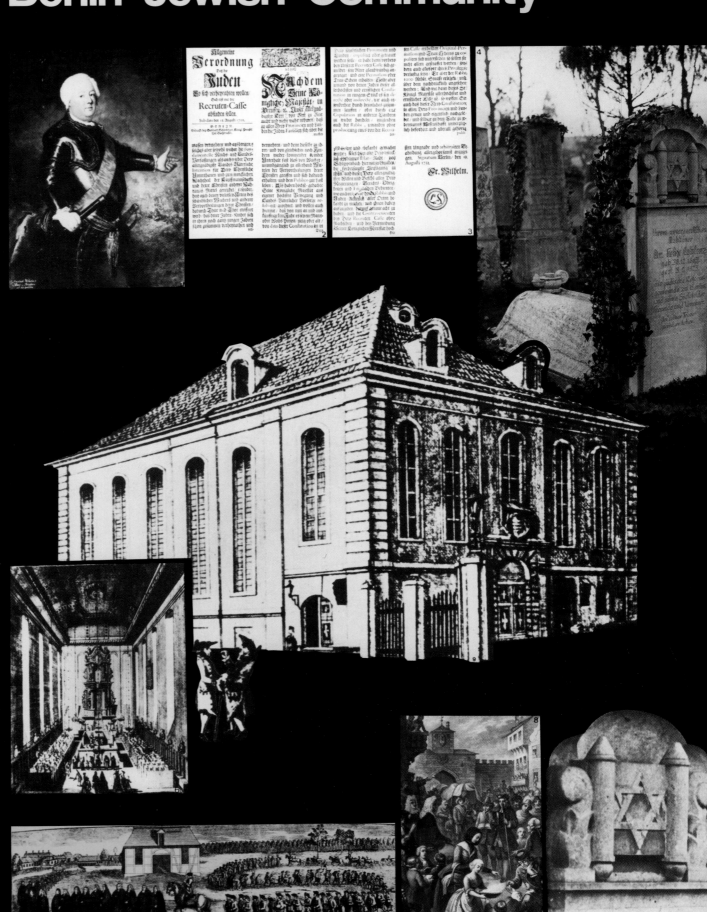

From 1708 to 1750 the Jews of Prussia were under the supervision of a permanent "Commission for the Jews." Jews had to contribute one-third of the Commission's cost. Edicts, orders and regulations (2,3) governed their lives.

Frederick William I (1) ascended the throne in 1713. One year later he attended the dedication of the first Berlin community synagogue on Heidereuthergasse (9: exterior; 6: interior). For the privilege to build this synagogue, the Jews had to pay the king 3,000 talers. The Jewish cemetery (4,5) on Grosse Hamburger Strasse had existed since 1672.

When Protestant refugees from Salzburg entered Berlin in 1732 (7,8), members of the Jewish community were among the first Berliners to offer aid to the fugitives.

The Usefulness Of "Privileged Jews"

In 1740 Frederick II, later known as Frederick the Great, became King of Prussia.

His Seven Years' War required all of the state's energies. After the Pyrrhic victory at the battle of Torgau in 1760 (1,2), Frederick II sent two Jewish merchants with a letter of recommendation (3) to the Crimean peninsula to buy horses for the Prussian army.

The king leased the Berlin mint to the Jew Daniel Itzig (5), holder of a "general privilege," and to the privileged Jew Veitel Ephraim, who in 1765 built himself a palatial mansion on Berlin's Molkenmarkt (7), one of the finest architectural structures in the city. These Jewish "court agents," together with the merchant Markus Levin (6), had the job of melting down valuable silver and striking coins made of inferior metal (copper with a silver surface) (4).

These "inflationary" measures enabled Frederick II to acquire part of the funds he needed for his wars. But the three Jews acquired a bad reputation:

"Outside, beauty; within, slime
Outside, Frederick; inside, Ephraim..."

went a popular verse.

Regulations

The special position of the Jews in a Christian society was governed by edicts.

Their economic potential was exploited, controlled and directed by privileges, regulations, letters of protection, etc.

The "General Privilege and Regulation," which Frederick William I had issued in 1730, was revised and tightened by Frederick II in 1750.

Frederick II And Tolerance

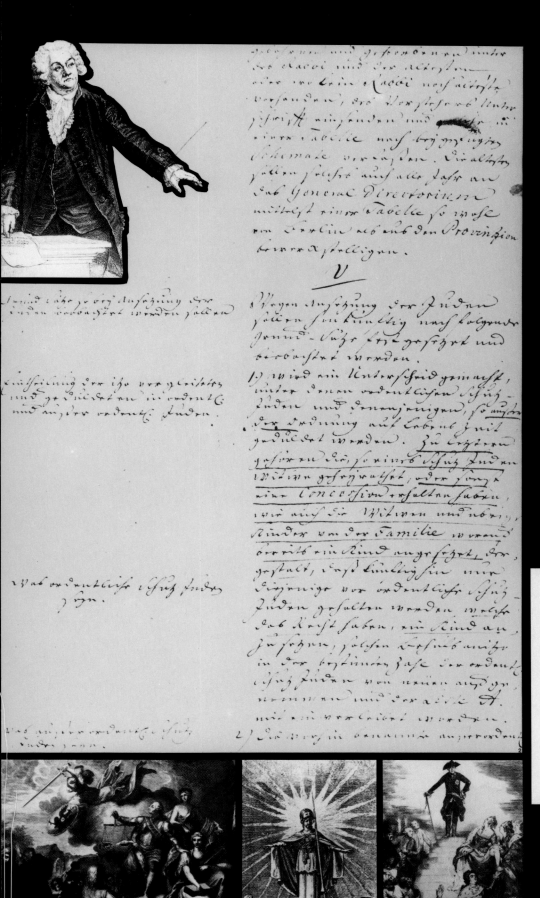

"All religions are equal," wrote Frederick II in the margin of a petition from a Catholic (3). His tolerance was glorified (4) and his sense of justice praised (6). One hundred years later, the painter Adolph Menzel still viewed him as the greatest among princes (5).

His policies toward the Jews, however, were not based on tolerance, nor on a humanistic spirit; they were determined primarily by economic considerations. By constantly increasing and imposing new taxes on the Jews of Prussia, Frederick II filled his empty treasury.

Ten years after his ascension to the throne, in 1750, he proclaimed the "Revised General Privilege and Rules for the Jewish Population in the Kingdom of Prussia" (2: hand-written draft of paragraph 2V).

In 1787 the French revolutionary Mirabeau (1) called it "a law worthy of a cannibal."

Moses Mendelssohn And His "Jewish Porcelain"

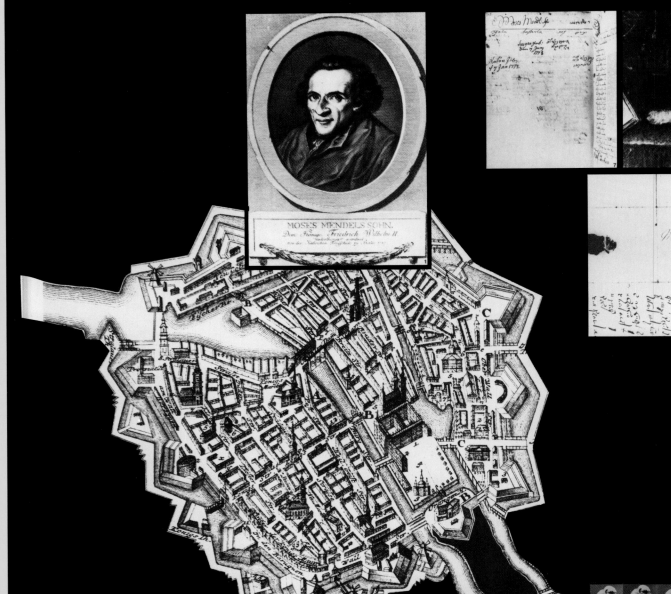

In the fall of 1743, the 14-year old Moses, son of the Tora-scribe Mendel of Dessau, entered the city of Berlin (2), probably by way of the Rosenthal Gate (4).

Every new arrival needed an entrance permit (3); Jews received their permit from a Jewish gatekeeper (6).

Moses Mendelssohn (1) married Fromet Gugenheim (5,8) in 1762.

In order to increase the business volume of the Berlin porcelain works which he had just purchased, Frederick II introduced in 1763 the following scheme: every Prussian Jew was forced, on such occasions as marriage, birth, death, business openings, purchases of a home, etc., to buy royal Prussian porcelain.

In this manner, probably in connection with the births of his children (7), Moses Mendelssohn in due course acquired a collection of twenty life-sized porcelain monkeys (9).

In 1787, one year after the death of Frederick II, his successor dropped this porcelain tax — in exchange for a tribute of 40,000 talers exacted from the Jews of Berlin.

Moses Mendelssohn (1729-1786)

"Here, in this so-called tolerant land, I live so hemmed in, so restricted on all sides by intolerance, that for the sake of my children, I must lock myself up in the silk factory all day long."
(Moses Mendelssohn, 1780)
Moses Mendelssohn was a bookkeeper, tutor, literary critic, Bible translator, co-owner of a factory, and philosopher. He was the first Jewish philosopher to interpret Judaism in the spirit of the Enlightenment.

1   In 1771 Frederick II ordered Moses Mendelssohn to come to Potsdam, but only because the chief minister of Saxony, von Fritsch, had requested Frederick II to do so. Frederick, however, did not receive Mendelssohn personally.
2   Dinner in the drawing room of Sanssouci Palace.
3   Immanuel Kant was a university lecturer in Koenigsberg when he received second prize, trailing Moses Mendelssohn, in a scholarly competition organized by the Royal Prussian Academy of Sciences in 1763.
4,5 Johann Kaspar Lavater, the Swiss theologian, visited Mendelssohn in order to convert him.
6-9 Gotthold Ephraim Lessing used his friend Moses Mendelssohn as a model for his character Nathan in the 1797 play "Nathan the Wise".

10ff Friedrich Nicolai, in his own right a writer and man of the Enlightenment, published the writings of Lessing and Mendelssohn.
15 Salomon Maimon (1754-1800) came to Berlin in 1780 and joined Mendelssohn's circle. With his "Essay Concerning Transcendental Philosophy" (1790) he contributed to the further development of Kantian philosophy.

Nathan der Weise.

Ein

Dramatisches Gedicht,

in fünf Aufzügen.

Introite, nam et heic Dii funt!
APVD GELLIVM.

Von

Gotthold Ephraim Leſſing.

Mit Churfürſtl. Sächſiſchem Privilegio.

Berlin,
bey Chriſtian Friedrich Voß und Sohn,
1779.

Friar: Nathan! You are a Christian,
by God, you are a Christian!
There never was a better one!
Nathan: So be it! For that which makes
me a Christian in your eyes, makes you
a Jew in mine!

("Nathan the Wise", Act 4, Scene 7)

After The Death Of Moses Mendelssohn

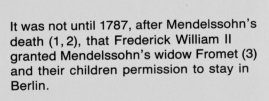

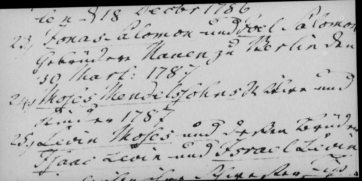

It was not until 1787, after Mendelssohn's death (1, 2), that Frederick William II granted Mendelssohn's widow Fromet (3) and their children permission to stay in Berlin.

Four of the six children converted to Christianity, including Abraham (6) and his wife, Lea (5). Abraham also had his children baptised. To his daughter Fanny (7) he wrote in 1820:

"We brought you up as Christians, because Christianity is the faith of most civilized people and contains nothing which would distract you from the path of virtue, and even more so it will guide you towards love, obedience, tolerance, and resignation...."

Abraham and Lea were the parents of the composer Felix Mendelssohn Bartholdy. Their tombstones are located in a cemetery in Berlin (8).

Abraham's brother Joseph (9), a banker who financed Alexander von Humboldt's travels in South America, never abandoned the Jewish faith.

Lesebuch

für

Jüdische Kinder.

חברת חינוך נערים

Zum Besten der jüdischen Freyschule.

Berlin

in Commißion bey Christian Friedrich Voß und Sohn

1779.

David Friedländer
Stifter der jüdischen Freyschule
zu Berlin

French design influenced fashion and architecture in Prussia (1-3).

In the spirit of the Enlightenment, the Jewish Free School was founded in Berlin in 1778. Its founders were Isaac Daniel Itzig and David Friedlaender (5); the school taught Western culture to Jewish children, using the German as well as the Hebrew alphabet (4,6).

An Enlightener Produces A Manifesto

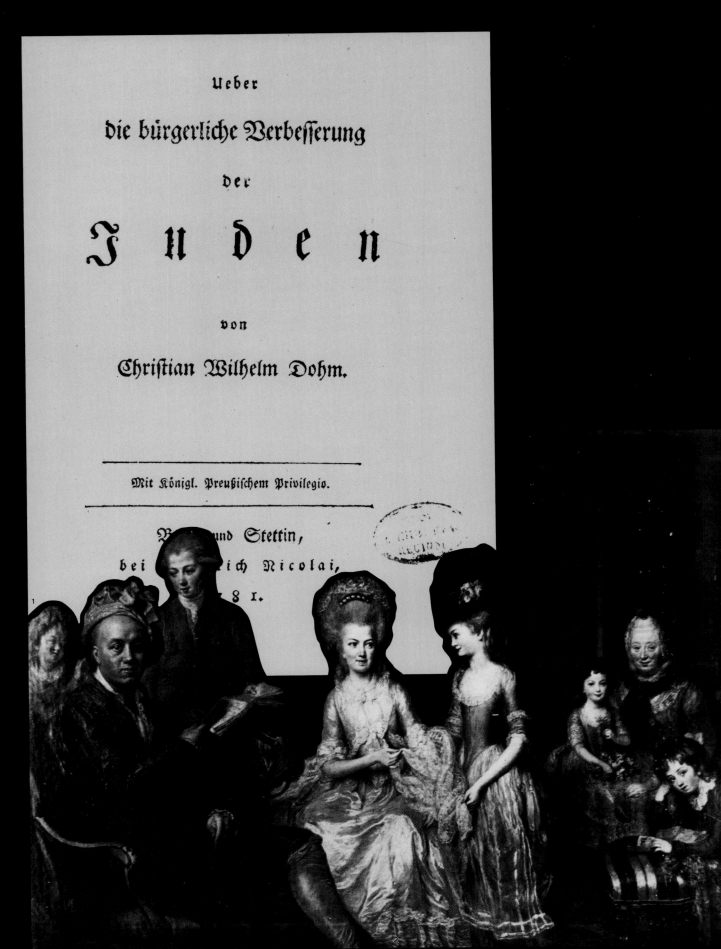

Ueber

die bürgerliche Verbesserung

der

Juden

von

Christian Wilhelm Dohm.

———

Mit Königl. Preußischem Privilegio.

———

B… und Stettin,

bei …ich Nicolai,

…8 1.

The Prussian military counsellor and archivist Christian Wilhelm Dohm, like Mendelssohn and Nicolai, whose home he often visited (2), was among the leaders of the Enlightenment in Berlin. His treatise (1) gave rise to lively discussions, even in Paris and Vienna:

"A Jew is more a human being than a Jew; how is it possible that he should not love a state in which he could freely acquire property and enjoy the free use of it, a state where he would not be taxed more heavily than other citizens and where he, too, could achieve honour and respect?"

Encounters In Salons

Early in the 19th century, in imitation of the French, the Berlin drawing rooms of Rahel Levin-Varnhagen (1), Henriette Herz (3), and Dorothea Schlegel (4), née Mendelssohn, became a meeting ground, where Jews and non-Jews discussed literary and aesthetic topics.

In these drawing rooms of the bourgeoisie (2) men and women felt that they were cosmopolitans, freed from religious and social ties.

"Precisely because the Jews were outsiders, the salons served, for a short time, as a sort of neutral territory where the educated could meet," wrote Hannah Arendt.

Among the visitors were Johann Gottlieb Fichte (5), Heinrich Heine (6), Karl August Varnhagen von Ense (7), Leopold von Ranke (8), Prince Louis Ferdinand (9), Wilhelm von Humboldt (10), Bettina von Arnim (11), Friedrich Gentz (12), Friedrich Hitzig (13), Georg Wilhelm Friedrich Hegel (14), Friedrich Heinrich Karl de la Motte Fouqué (15), Ludwig Tieck (16), Heinrich von Kleist (17), Friedrich Schleiermacher (18), Johann Gottfried Schadow (19), Alexander von Humboldt (20), Adelbert von Chamisso (21), Adam Mueller (22), Prince Pueckler-Muskau (23), Jean Paul (24), and Eduard Gans (25).

Forerunners Of Modern Anti-Semitism

In 1793 Fichte had already recommended "cutting off all Jewish heads one night and replacing them with others which contain not a single Jewish idea. To protect ourselves from them, I see no other means but to conquer their Holy Land for them and to send them all back there."

Eisenmenger, der Zweite.

Nebst

einem vorangesetzten Sendschreiben

an

den Herrn Professor Fichte

in Jena

von

S. Ascher.

metiri — quemque suo modulo ac pede
verum est.

Berlin, 1794.
Bey Carl Ludwig Hartmann.

Die

Germanomanie.

Skizze

zu

einem Zeitgemälde.

Von

S. Ascher,
Doktor der Philosophie.

Berlin, 1815.
Bei Achenwall und Comp.

Idee

einer

Preßfreiheit

und

Censurordnung.

Den

hohen Mitgliedern des Bundestages

vorgelegt.

Von

D. S. Ascher.

Leipzig,
bei Achenwall und Comp.
1818.

Die

Wartburgs = Feier.

Mit Hinsicht

auf

Deutschlands

religiöse und politische Stimmung.

Von

Dr. S. Ascher.

Leipzig, 1818.
Bei Achenwall und Comp.

Forerunners Of Modern Anti-Semitism

In 1811 Conservative politicians and Romantic poets created the "Christian-German Round Table" in Berlin.

Its most prominent members were Karl von Clausewitz (1), Heinrich von Kleist (2), Clemens Brentano (7), Friedrich Carl von Savigny (8), and Johann Gottlieb Fichte (9). Only "persons born in the Christian faith" were accepted; Jews and converts were barred. In this circle, Brentano referred to the Jews as "those flies who survived the Egyptian plagues."

The Berlin Jewish bookseller and writer Saul Ascher (1767-1822) protested against the anti-Semitic position of Fichte and his friends (3-6).

The Prussian Reforms

Following Napoleon's victory in 1806, the general political reforms implemented in Prussia also included the legal emancipation of Jews. State Chancellor Karl August Freiherr von Hardenberg, supported by Wilhelm von Humboldt, introduced the *Emancipation Edict* on March 11, 1812. According to this decree, the Jews became Prussian citizens with all rights and duties. The Jewish periodical *Sulamith* stated in 1812: *"March 11 marks the beginning of a happy new era for our fellow-Jews in the Prussian state."* This hope turned out to be an illusion.

The Wars of Liberation from 1813-1815 gave Jewish men for the first time the opportunity to prove how far they identified with the fate of Prussia. 170 Prussian Jews were drafted and many volunteered to fight against Napoleon.

From the Congress of Vienna to the 1848 Revolution

Napoleon's final defeat in 1815 and the subsequent Congress of Vienna was followed by the era of the Restoration. For the Jews of Prussia it meant a time of setbacks and restrictions. We read, for example, in an 1816 memorandum from the Prussian Ministry of Finances: *"It would be desirable not to have any Jews at all among us. Since we have them, however, we have to put up with them; but we must strive incessantly to render them as powerless as possible. The conversion of Jews to the Christian faith must be facilitated; all civil rights flow from that. But as long as the Jew remains a Jew, he cannot obtain a position in the state."*

At the same time the historian Friedrich Ruehs (1781-1820), published *On the Jewish Demands for Civil Rights*. It was the first in a series of anti-Jewish pamphlets demanding the suspension of the *Emancipation Edict* of 1812. Ruehs declared that the Jews were a *"peculiar nation"* and outsiders in the German-Christian state; as such, they were only entitled to the rights of aliens. He demanded the introduction of a *"Jews' tax"* and recommended that Jews should wear a distinctive sign identifying them as aliens.

Members of various Jewish communities thought that their assimilation had begun with the Edict of 1812 and reacted to their emancipation with demands for internal reforms. These additional reforms were supposed to diminish their national and cultural peculiarities and thus integrate their community as a religious body into the German nation. This was based on the idea that according to the *Emancipation Edict* of 1812, the Jews were to consider Prussia their homeland. David Friedlaender (1750-1834), one of the officials of the Berlin Jewish community, as well as his successors, urged reform of religious services and education. The service was to be conducted in German instead of Hebrew, and all references to yearning for the faraway homeland of Zion were to be deleted.

Until the end of the 19th century, Jews acted as individuals but never as a group promoting their political interests. Excluded from civil service positions prior to the 1848 revolution, political and literary activity remained the only possibility to participate in and influence public life.

Johann Jacoby (1805-1877) of Koenigsberg wrote: *"As I am simultaneously a Jew and a German, the Jew in me cannot be liberated without the German, and the German in me cannot be liberated without the Jew. As I cannot divide myself, I cannot separate one freedom from the other."* Jacoby was an ardent supporter of the ideas of the French Revolution; he maintained that only the development of democratic ideals and the extension of general civil rights could realize the emancipation of the Jews. The Jewish problem did not preoccupy his political activities because he believed that the creation of a democratic climate would also solve this question.

The writers Ludwig Boerne (1786-1837) and Heinrich Heine (1797-1856) held similiar views and exercised great influence on the political-literary opposition during the pre-revolutionary period. Heine hoped to join the Prussian Civil Service after completing his doctorate in jurisprudence. Although he converted to Protestantism in 1825, he still did not obtain the desired position.

While individual Jewish politicians, publicists, and journalists participated in various political groups, most Jews remained only passive sympathizers with the liberal forces. A relatively large number of Jewish citizens took part in the struggles of the revolution of 1848, particularly in Berlin, Breslau, and Koenigsberg.

The demand that civil rights should be independent of religion, as expressed in the *Ordinance Concerning the Fundamentals of a Future Prussian Constitution* (April 6, 1848), seemed to satisfy the demand for the legal emancipation of the Jews. The failure of the 1848 Revolution resulted in restrictions on general political activity and in a setback for the Jewish emancipation.

Traders And Peddlers

Since the Middle Ages Jews had been denied ownership of land, participation in agricultural activities, and access to the guild-controlled crafts.

Pawnbrokerage, cattle dealing, the unregulated small-scale trade in second-hand goods and clothes, and house-to-house peddling were the main livelihoods by which they maintained themselves.

Their chances to make a living were restricted; their social position was defined and marked for centuries.

Napoleon And Jewish Emancipation

Between 1806 and 1815 the map of Prussia changed three times. Napoleon's march through the Brandenburg Gate (1) into Berlin in 1806, and the occupation of the Prussian capital by French troops (2), spelled the end of the old Prussia. In her former western territories, ceded in the peace of Tilsit, the Jews were emancipated as a result of the French Revolution.

In March 1813 Frederick William III appealed to his people "to take up arms for the liberation of Prussia" (3).

For the first time, 170 Prussian Jews, made full citizens by the edict of 1812, were drafted (4); 561 Jewish citizens volunteered and fought for Prussia's freedom (5, 6).

Meno Burg (1787-1853) was the first jewish Royal Prussian Major of the Artillery (7).

The Emancipation Edict Of 1812

Prussia after the Third Polish Partition (1795)
Prussia after the Peace of Tilsit (1807)
Prussia after the Congress of Vienna (from 1815)

Equal rights for the Jews were first proclaimed in Prussia within a framework of general reforms after Napoleon's victory over the Prussians. Chancellor Karl August von Hardenberg (1), with the support of Alexander von Humboldt and others, issued a bill giving equal rights to the Jews of Prussia — the Emancipation Edict of March 11, 1812 (3, 4). Karl Freiherr vom Stein (2) opposed the reform.

The Edict declared that Jews were citizens and imposed on them the same duties as on all other citizens. As Prussian citizens, they could now freely chose their professions.

Their admittance into the higher ranks of the military and the civil service, however, was to be regulated at a later date. They were forced to adopt "firmly established family names" and to use the German language or another modern language for their accounts, contracts, etc.

"As of March 11, a new happy era has begun for our fellow-Jews in the Prussian states," proclaimed the Jewish journal "Sulamith" in 1812.

These hopes proved to be illusory. The edict applied solely to those Jews who held "Letters of Protection" and concessions in the four provinces of Brandenburg, Silesia, Pomerania, and East Prussia.

After Napoleon's final defeat in 1815, the Congress of Vienna (5) implemented the Age of Restoration, and a period of setbacks for the Jews of Prussia followed.

In 1816 a statement by the Prussian Ministry of Finance noted: "It would be desirable not to have any Jews at all among us. Since we have them, however, we have to put up with them; but we must strive incessantly to render them as powerless as possible. The conversion of Jews to the Christian faith must be facilitated; all civil rights flow from that. But as long as the Jew remains a Jew, he cannot obtain a position in the state."

Victory Over Napoleon

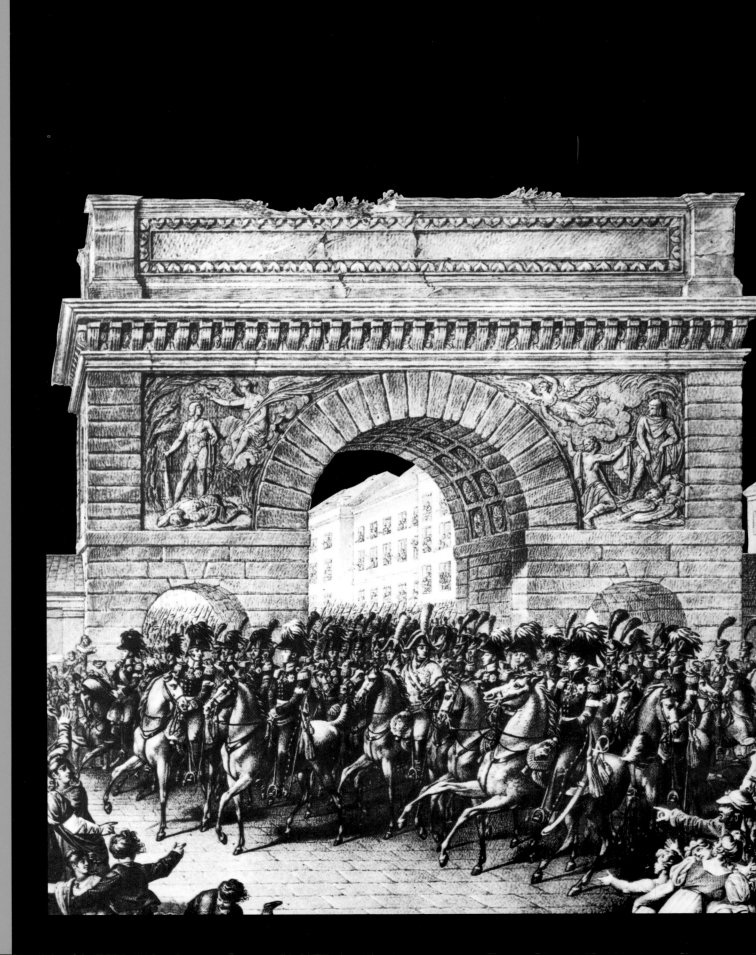

The war ended with the arrival of the allied armies of Prussia, Russia and Austria in Paris, March 31, 1814 (8).

In Search Of A Definition

Between the years 1842 and 1846, 7 out of every 1,000 Berlin Jews were baptized, between 1847 and 1856 every 2.2, and between 1867 and 1871 only 0.8.

After obtaining the doctorate of juris-prudence, Heinrich Heine (1) set his hopes on a position in the Prussian civil service. In 1825 he decided to be baptized as a Protestant. Yet he did not get any appointment. His comment is well-known: "The baptismal certificate is the ticket of admission to European culture." In 1826 he wrote to his friend Moses Moser: "Now I am hated by both Jews and Christians. I regret very much that I decided to be baptized." His famous poem "Loreley" (2) was published in 1824.

For those Jews who did not intend to become Christians, but still surrendered their Jewish national identity in exchange for German culture and their Jewish traditions for European culture, Judaism had to be defined anew. Judaism was to become a subject of modern research and teaching in order to preserve its spiritual existence. This was the aim of Leopold Zunz (3; his wife Adelheid 4), Moses Moser, and Eduard Gans (5), who in 1819 founded the "Society for Culture and Science of Judaism" and published the "Journal for Studies in Judaism" which for a time counted Heinrich Heine among its contributors. Among the founders, it was above all Zunz who influenced the next generation of students of Judaism, i.e. Samson Raphael Hirsch (6), Zacharias Frankel (7), and Heymann Steinthal (8).

In 1869 Abraham Geiger (r) and Moritz Lazarus (c), together with the president of the Vienna Jewish congregation, Baron von Wertheimer (l), were elected chairmen of the first Synod in Leipzig (9).

Freedom In Chains

The forces of restoration which had prevailed in Europe following the Congress of Vienna resisted the progressive movement in Prussia and thus created impediments to the process of Jewish emancipation. Liberal tendencies were suppressed, civil rights curtailed.

The resolutions of the Karlsbad Conference in 1819 (1), attended by the reactionary Austrian Chancellor Metternich (4), the Prussian King Frederick William III (2), his Chancellor Hardenberg, and the ministers Wittgenstein and Bernstorff, reintroduced press censorship (3) and suppressed all free expression of opinion.

Growth Of Industrialization

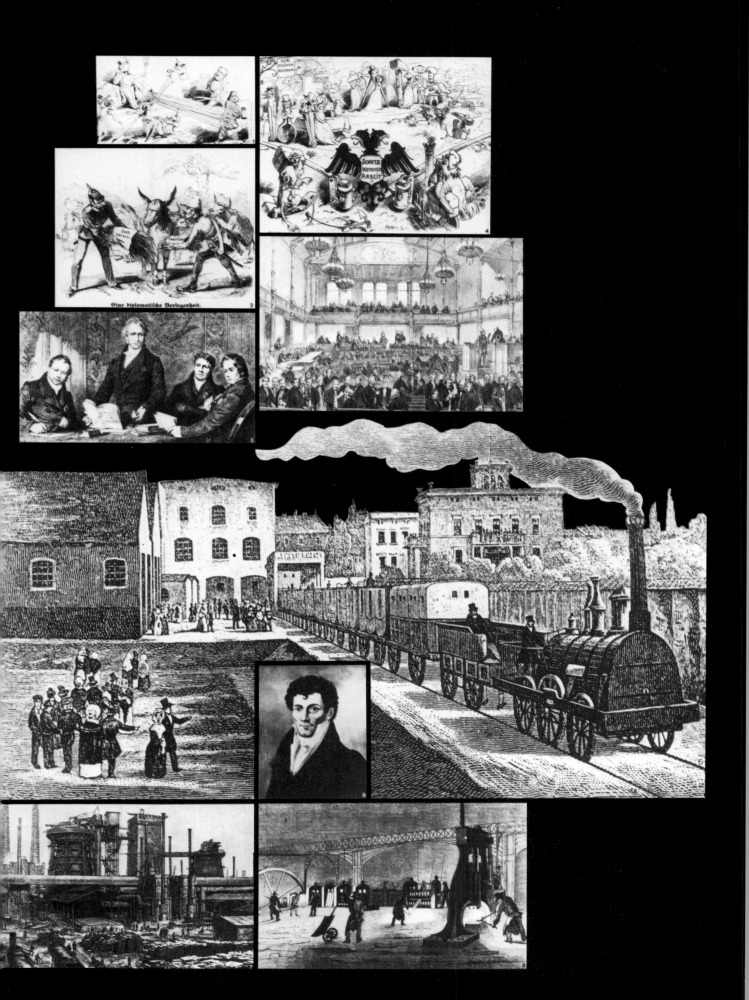

Between 1819 and 1828, Prussia entered into customs agreements with the neighbouring small states; the German Customs Union was founded in 1834. An economic union of most German states was hereby achieved which favoured the development of industry and commerce. 1868 saw the creation of the Customs Parliament which reformed the custom and tax laws.

1 "German customs manoeuvres," a cartoon about protective tariffs
2 "Diplomatic embarrassment," a cartoon about the German Customs Union and the bait offered to the small states
3 The founders of the German Customs Union:
   Friedrich von Motz, Karl von Massen, Wilhelm von Klewitz, Friedrich von Eichhorn
4 "Protection of German labour," cartoon against the protective tariff
5 Chamber of the German Customs Parliament in Berlin

Jews were better prepared to cope with the new system of competition and its results than other social groups. This advantage gave them a favourable start in the industrial economy (7, 8).

The railway line Berlin-Potsdam (6) was financed by Levin Arons (9).

Romanticism — A German Invention

With its spiritual return to the past and the Middle Ages, and its overemphasis on sentimentality, Romanticism, a reaction to rational thinking, provided the ideals for bourgeois conservative thought.

Jewish participation in bourgeois Romanticism was modest. Glorification of the past would have been tantamount to glorification of life in the ghetto. Jews stood at the opposite end of the intellectual spectrum and were committed to social change.

Rebellion And The Textile Industry

The Jews played a pioneering role in Prussia's industrialization.

In the textile sector small businesses could be kept alive only by adapting to new technical developments (1). The cotton industry (2, 3) was rapidly mechanized. In 1824 the Silesian textile manufacturer Meyer Kauffmann and his wife Philippine (7, 8) established a draper's shop in Schweidnitz.
In 1841 they opened a branch in Breslau. After the London Exposition of 1851, they purchased 200 mechanical looms and opened a textile factory (9).

"It soon became clear that the sale of goods to printers and finishers did not yield sufficient return; for that reason, we decided to bleach and dye our own cotton fabrics and to sell the products, together with hand-made goods, at fairs and through travelling salesmen, to the retail trade" (Salomon Kauffmann).

The mechanization of the industry caused the prices of finished products to fall.

The textile manufacturers cut the weavers' wages, thus reducing them to dire poverty (6). The rebellion of the Silesian weavers in June 1844 (4), the first proletarian revolt in Prussia, was put down by military forces (5).

The Debate About A Future Constitution

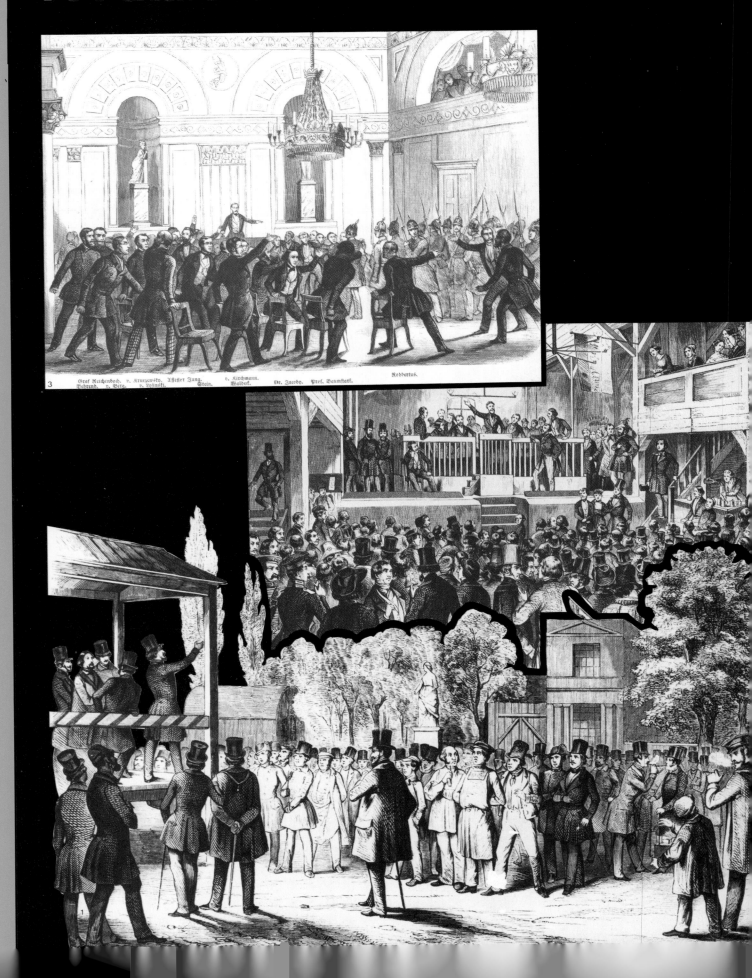

The resolutions of the Frankfurt
National Assembly and of the Prussian
Constitutional Assembly were publicly
discussed in the Berlin Tiergarten (1)
and in political clubs (2). In November
1848 the Constitutional Assembly was
dissolved by the Prussian army (3).

The Memorable Years, 1848/1849

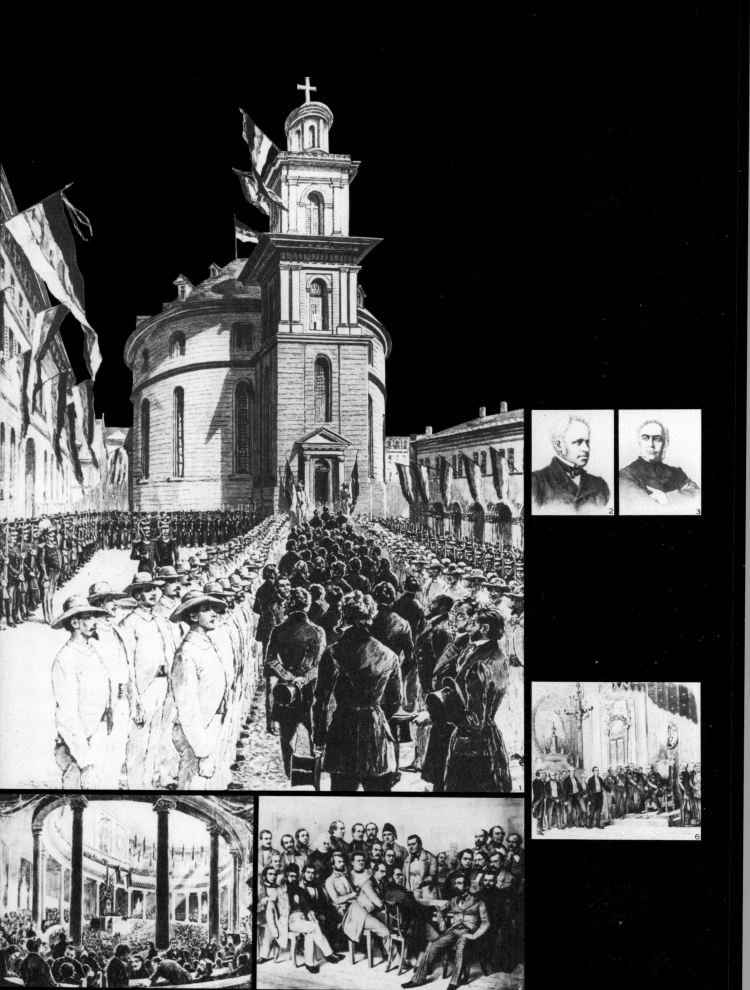

On March 30, 1848 the members of the preliminary parliament entered St. Paul's Church in Frankfurt (1). Among the 586 deputies were seven Prussian Jews, including the Berlin publisher Moritz Veit (2), and the future president of the assembly, the Koenigsberg lawyer Eduard Simson (3). The Frankfurt parliament (4, 5) drafted an all-German constitution.

A deputation in April 1849, headed by Eduard Simson offered the Prussian king the imperial crown in the Knight's Hall of the Royal Palace in Berlin (6). The king refused.

"...The Misfortune Of Kings...."

"As I myself am a Jew as well as a German, the Jew in me cannot be free without the German; the German cannot be free without the Jew," wrote the Koenigsberg physician and politician Johann Jacoby (4). It was his conviction that Jewish emancipation was possible only in a constitutional state and the achievement of democratic conditions would of itself lead to a solution of the "Jewish question." He appealed to King Frederick William IV of Prussia (1) with the words: "It is the misfortune of kings that they do not wish to hear the truth!" (2) As one of the leaders of the radical opposition he formulated, in his "Four Questions Answered by an East Prussian" of 1841, the demand for a Prussian constitution:

1. What do the estates want?
    Legally secured participation of the free citizens in the affairs of the state.
2. What is the justification for this demand?
    The awareness of their political maturity and the actual and legal proclamation thereof on May 22, 1815.
3. What answer did the estates receive?
    Recognition of their loyalty, repudiation of the demands presented and soothing references to a future undefined substitution.
4. What can the assembly do now?
    To claim as a demonstrated right that which we used to plead for as a favour.

In March 1848 revolutionary struggle came to Berlin. Barricades were built in the streets (6). Pamphlets which warned of an impending civil war were published in German-Yiddish dialect (5). Prussian troops sent bullets against Prussian citizens (7,9).

Two hundred and thirty fatalities were the result. The dead were lined up in state (10). Among them were 21 Jews for whom prayers were said by Rabbi Michael Sachs (8).

On the occasion of the fiftieth anniversary of the revolution, the physician and statesman Julius Moses proposed in 1897 without success the erection of a monument to the fallen (11).

"I Am No Enemy Of The Jews"

Ernst ist das Leben, heiter ist die Kunst. 5

Bismarck's (1) attitude towards the Jews was ambiguous. On the eve of the revolution of 1848, he had argued in the Prussian United Assembly (4) against legal equality of the Jews:

"I am no enemy of the Jews: indeed, I love them under certain conditions. I would also like them to have every conceivable right, except the one to an administrative post in a Christian nation."

He was a friend of the Jewish Berlin Opera soprano Pauline Lucca (2); while at the Bad Ischl spa he was photographed in her company (5). The Jewish banker Gerson Bleichroeder (3) was his financial advisor.

During his tenure as Chancellor of the North German Federation, legal equality of the Jews was secured by the law of 1869.

As Chancellor of the newly created German Reich, he answered attacks by the Conservative "Kreuzzeitung" in 1875 as follows: "In their opposition to me, the Jews have never been as base as my Christian adversaries."

In spite of anti-Semitism the Jewish upper and middle classes strove for assimilation (14, 15).

In 1824 the mathematician David Unger, who had become a Prussian citizen (9) two years before, applied for a post as an instructor at the Academy of Architecture, supported by a letter of recommendation from the lawyer and philosopher Eduard Gans (10, 11). Frederick William III refused the application and personally informed Unger, that he could apply again after his conversion to Protestantism (12).

In 1841 a Jewish "home owner" became a citizen of Berlin: Martin Valentin (6), his wife Rosa (7), and his "Letter of Citizenship"(8).

Occasionally, Jews were received at court (13) and invited to the White Hall (2) of the Royal Palace in Berlin (1).

The new synagogue in Oranienburgerstrasse was designed by the Protestant architect Eduard Knoblauch. On September 5, 1866 Prime Minister Bismarck and his cabinet attended the opening ceremony. The synagogue had 3,000 seats and was considered one of the most beautiful in Europe (3, 4).

Königsberg

Danzig

Preußen
37.635

Pommern
12.488

Posen
74.172

Die jüdische Bevölkerung in
den preußischen Provinzen (1863)

Schlesien
40.856

Breslau

14

15

Little more than 1% of the population in 1870 was Jewish. The majority of Jews lived in Berlin, Posen, and Silesia.

The number of Jews in the Prussian provinces (1863):

Brandenburg	=	Brandenburg	30,694
Pommern	=	Pommerania	12,488
Posen	=	Posen	74,172
Preussen	=	Prussia	37,665
Rheinland	=	Rhineland	34,248
Sachsen	=	Saxony	5,775
Schlesien	=	Silesia	40,856
Westfalen	=	Westphalia	16,631

The Road To Scientific Socialism

Moses Hess (2), co-founder and editor of the "Rheinische Zeitung," looked for a solution to the Jewish question first of all through a reform of society's class structure.

In his book "Rome and Jerusalem" (1) he later argued, that the Jewish people ought to have a state of their own.

"The Social-Democrat" (3) was the organ of the "General German Workers' Association" (4, 8, 10) founded by Ferdinand Lassalle (5). In its statutes (7), the Association supported the general, equal, and direct right to vote as basic for a just representation of the political interests of the working class. Karl Marx (6), son of a converted Jewish lawyer, became the founder of scientific socialism. In his main work, "Das Kapital" (9), he analyses capitalist society and the laws behind its development.

After 1866 Bismarck fought hard in the Prussian House of Representatives for the support of the newly founded National Liberal Party for which a majority of the Jewish citizenry had cast its vote.

Eduard Lasker (6), successful lawyer, liberal politician, and member of the Reichstag (1, 2, 3, 4) whose support, according to a contemporary caricature (8), was of great importance to Bismarck.

Eduard Simson, president of the North German Reichstag who was elevated to the nobility 21 years later, opening a session in 1867 (7).

Lasker, together with the deputy Ludwig Bamberger (5), a long-time advisor of Bismarck in matters of free trade, left the party in 1880 because of its support of Bismarck's anti-socialist laws and the Chancellor's protective tariffs policies.

Legal Equalitiy For The Jews Of Prussia

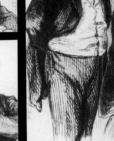

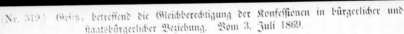

(Nr. 319.) Gesetz, betreffend die Gleichberechtigung der Konfessionen in bürgerlicher und staatsbürgerlicher Beziehung. Vom 3. Juli 1869.

Wir Wilhelm, von Gottes Gnaden König von Preußen ꝛc.

verordnen im Namen des Norddeutschen Bundes, nach erfolgter Zustimmung des Bundesrathes und des Reichstages, was folgt:

Einziger Artikel.

Alle noch bestehenden, aus der Verschiedenheit des religiösen Bekenntnisses hergeleiteten Beschränkungen der bürgerlichen und staatsbürgerlichen Rechte werden hierdurch aufgehoben. Insbesondere soll die Befähigung zur Theilnahme an der Gemeinde- und Landesvertretung und zur Bekleidung öffentlicher Aemter vom religiösen Bekenntniß unabhängig sein.

Urkundlich unter Unserer Höchsteigenhändigen Unterschrift und beigedrucktem Bundes-Insiegel.

Gegeben Schloß Babelsberg, den 3. Juli 1869.

(L. S.) Wilhelm.

Gr. v. Bismarck-Schönhausen.

The North German Federation was founded in 1867 when the North German states joined together under the leadership of Prussia (1). The first elections in accordance with the general election law took place in February of that year (2, 3, 5, 6).

The Federation represented an intermediate stage on the road to the creation of the Empire. In 1868 the Prussian King William I received the Federation's ministers in Berlin (7). The Federation seal showed the heraldic shields of the 22 member states.

The legal equality of the Jews can be dated back to the law of July 3, 1869 (4).

On July 9, 1870 Bismarck presented the declaration of war against France to the parliament of the North German Federation (8).

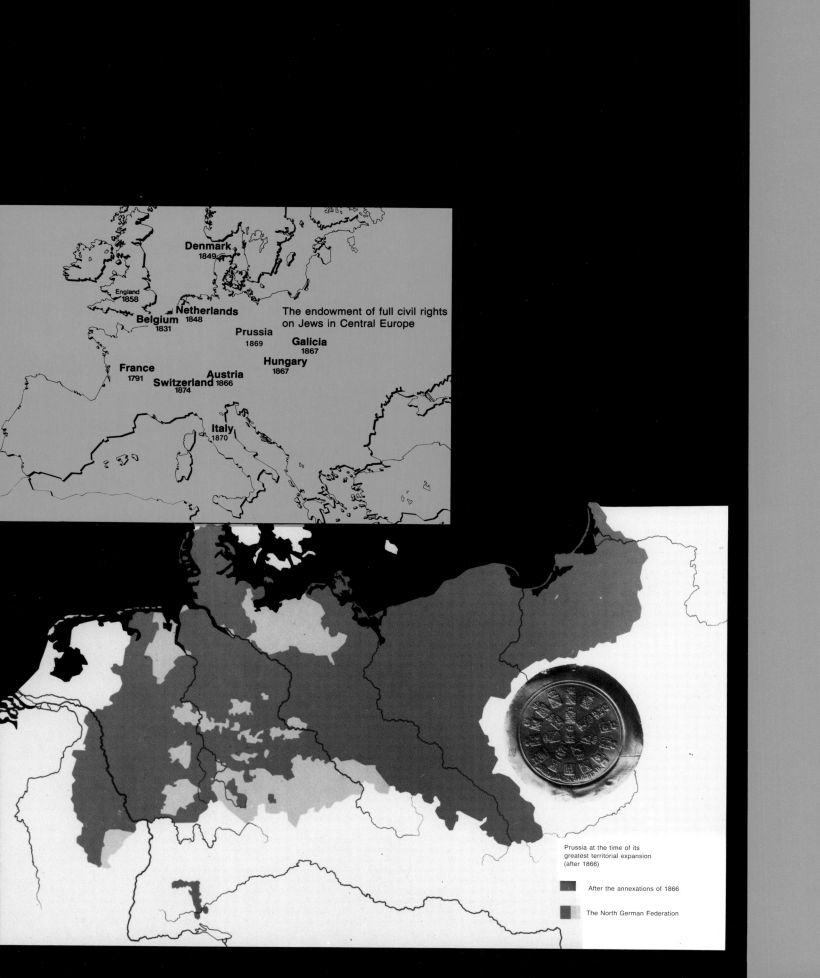

Denmark
1849

England
1858

Netherlands
1848

Belgium
1831

Prussia
1869

Galicia
1867

The endowment of full civil rights
on Jews in Central Europe

France
1791

Austria
1866

Switzerland
1874

Hungary
1867

Italy
1870

Prussia at the time of its
greatest territorial expansion
(after 1866)

After the annexations of 1866

The North German Federation

The Empire:
An Experiment in Assimilation

The National Constitution of 1871 finally realized the emancipation for all religions. Yet, in spite of equality under the law, discrimination continued on a social basis. Just as before, Jews found civil service positions, with few exceptions, closed and full professorships at universities were rarely awarded to them.

The very prestigious position of a reserve officer also remained closed to Jews in Prussia but not in Bavaria.

The history of Prussian Jews in the 19th century is closely linked to the growing industrialization and the capitalistic system. Trade and transportation, traditional Jewish enterprises, grew in importance. The social status of the Jewish population rose accordingly and significant numbers adopted the norms of the German middle class.

Initially, the majority of the Jewish middle class joined the liberal parties. During the first few years after the establishment of the Empire, about 70 percent of the Prussian Jews voted for the National Liberal Party. Jewish writers, artists, philosophers, and scientists took part in the cultural life of the country without stressing their Jewishness. Due to gradual assimilation Judaism seemed to lose its central meaning.

Against the backdrop of Jewish emancipation anti-Semitism took on new characteristics.

The conservative and reactionary anti-Semitic groups accused the Jews of being the main culprits of the *Great Depression* (1873-1896). The economic success of many Jews enabled the anti-Semites to represent them as symbols of the modern economic system and to hold the Jews responsible for all the negative manifestations of a rapidly changing society. Thus anti-Semitism after 1880 became a tenet of a number of political parties.

The Social Democrats, who suffered under the anti-Socialist Law (1878-1890), opposed anti-Semitism. They viewed anti-Semitism as an integral part of capitalistic society. The Social Democratic Party's stand against all forms of discrimination attracted a fair number of Jewish politicians to the Party. Of the twenty-six Jewish members of the *Reichstag* (national parliament) between 1893 and 1918, seventeen belonged to the Social Democratic Party, four were left-wing liberals, another four National Liberals, and one belonged to a conservative faction.

Anti-Jewish ideas merged with racist ideology. The Social Darwinist doctrine, lauding the victory of the stronger nation over the weaker one, was fused with religious resentment against the Jews. By ascribing exclusively negative, unalterable, racial characteristics to the Jews, the ideas of the Enlightenment and of liberalism were refuted.

In 1879 the historian Heinrich von Treitschke *(The Jews are our misfortune)*, and the Protestant theologian and court chaplain Adolf Stoecker were the first to appeal to the public with anti-Semitic statements. These men greatly contributed to furthering anti-Semitism among the middle classes.

Growing anti-Semitism reminded Jewish citizens that their full integration into society was not yet a fact. The threat of anti-Semitism created a new feeling of community among the Jews, and their drive to attain civil rights gained momentum. During the years following the establishment of the Empire, the Jews tried to realize their goal of equal social status by supporting political and social organizations. Threatened by political anti-Semitism, they tried to obtain their rights by forming Jewish associations and coalitions. From 1890 to 1910 twenty-four Jewish organizations were founded. Despite anti-Semitism, the majority of German Jewry followed the path of assimilation. They sought acceptance as German citizens of the Jewish faith.

Only a minority of Jews chose not to take that path and joined the newly established Zionist movement. Its primary aim was *the establishment of a legal and secure home in Palestine* for all Jews. According to Richard Lichtheim, Zionism begins *"where the ideas of modern times, that is the Enlightenment philosophy of the 18th century and the movements of national liberation of the 19th century, link up for the first time with the thousand-year-old yearning for Zion.... Inasmuch as Zionism is not rooted in a religious-national myth, it is a gift from Europe, namely the application first of the idea of the civil and, then, of the national emancipation of the Jews."* Between 1905 and 1914 Berlin was the center of the Zionist World Movement.

"Elevated By Faith, Encouraged To Do His Duty"

In the Franco-Prussian War of 1870/71, Jewish soldiers were the equals of their Christian comrades.

They fought at Sedan (1), celebrated Yom Kippur at Metz (2), remembered their fallen comrades at Woerth (4).

Jewish women received medals for the nursing of the wounded (5). The Jewish press celebrated the reestablishment of a German Empire (3).

Prussia's King William I was proclaimed German Emperor in Versailles on January 18, 1871 (6).

With the acceleration of social change problems of transition became more pressing. The tensions between the Jews and the pre-bourgeois and pre-industrial elements of the ruling system increased sharply. In the political arena a rapid weakening of the position of the Liberals occurred, with an obvious turn toward a conservative and authoritarian paternalistic state. The rise of modern German anti-Semitism developed out of this situation. An attempt was made to explain the crisis of middle-class society as caused by the activities of the Jews; the crisis was to be overcome by the repudiation of their emancipation.

Sports — A National Movement

Freudenfeuer der Turner auf dem Kreu am 1 Jahrestage der Schlacht bei Lei Vater Jahn hält die Ansprache

In contrast to other countries, sports in Germany had patriotic origins. After the severe defeat of the Prussian forces at Jena and Auerstedt in 1806, the young were filled with enthusiasm for the idea of physical training. Friedrich Ludwig Jahn (1) set the pace on the playing field in Berlin (2). On the occasion of the first anniversary of Napoleon's decisive defeat at the Battle of Leipzig, he gave the main address (3).

At the first modern Olympics in Athens in 1896, the 27-year old Alfred Flatow (4, on left) received Germany's first medal in gymnastics for his achievements on the parallel bars; he also received a second medal for his performance on the horizontal bar. Under Hitler, he was deported and perished in 1942 in Theresienstadt.

Around the turn of the century, German Jewish sports clubs such as the Maccabi organization and the Bar Kochba student athletics club (5) were formed.

"The Jews Are Our Misfortune"

Heinrich von Treitschke (2), professor of history in Berlin, wrote in 1879: "Even in circles of the noblest erudition and among men who would reject with horror any thought of clerical intolerance or national arrogance, it is now said as with one voice: the Jews are our misfortune."

His colleague Theodor Mommsen (8) replied in 1880: "There you have the real centre of the lunacy which is now gripping the masses, and von Treitschke is its prophet."

Adolf Stoecker (1), court chaplain in Berlin, said in 1883: "We challenge the Jews to do battle until total victory, and we will not rest until they have been plunged into the dust where they belong."

Anti-Semitism became a mass movement and a component of German patriotism.

A medieval prejudice was resurrected and "dressed in the cloak of idealism." It was expressed in print by Hermann Ahlwardt (3), principal of a Berlin grammar school and member of the Reichstag, and by the philosopher Eugen Duehring (4) in his book "The Jewish Question as a Question of Race, Custom, and Culture."

Anti-Semitism became "the most foolproof means to control the emotions of the masses" and poisoned the every-day life of society (6, 7).

Professors like Theodor Mommsen (8), Rudolf Virchow (9), and Johann Gustav Droysen (10) protested sharply against Treitschke and Stoecker, but to no avail.

The word Zionism was first coined in Germany by Nathan Birnbaum in 1893. It was formally accepted by Theodor Herzl (1860-1904) (15) and the first Zionist Congress (16), in Basel (1897).

In 1895 the first Zionist monthly (1) was published in Berlin.

According to Richard Lichtheim (10), president of the Zionist Organization in Germany from 1917 to 1920, Zionism begins "at the point where the ideas of modern times, that is the Enlightenment philosophy of the 18th century and the movements of national liberation of the 19th century, link up for the first time with the thousand-year-old yearning for Zion.... Inasmuch as Zionism is not rooted in a religious-national myth, it is a gift from Europe, namely the application first of the idea of the civil and, then, of the national emancipation of the Jews."

Students founded the "Russian-Jewish-Scientific Club" in Berlin in 1889. A group photo was taken in 1890 (2). Standing from left to right are Simha Rosenbloom, unidentified, Michael Vrosenstein, Victor Jacobson, Schmarya Levin, Joseph Luria, and Nachman Syrkin. Seated from left to right are Israel Motzkin, Heinrich Loewe, and Leo Motzkin.

In 1902 the "Juedischer Verlag" was founded in Berlin (3). This publishing house was for many years the leading Zionist Press. Its founders were Martin Buber (seated, right); his friend Berthold Feiwel (seated, left); Ephraim Moshe Lilien, Chajim Weizmann, and Davis Trietsch (standing, left to right).

Another group photo from 1902 shows the members of the German Zionist delegation which visited the Grand Duke of Baden on the occasion of the 50th anniversary of his ascension to the throne (4). From left to right: Alfred Klee, Julius Moses, Max Bodenheimer, Rudolf Schauer, Adolf Friedemann, and Max Kaufmann.

Leading Zionists included, among others, the lawyer Max Bodenheimer (5), the lumber dealer David Wolffsohn (6), the physician and editor Max Jungmann (7), the lawyer and politician Adolf Friedemann (8), the lawyer Felix Rosenblueth (9), later Israel's Minister of Justice, the physician and economist Franz Oppenheimer (11), the editor Kurt Blumenfeld (12), and the lawyer and politician Arthur Hantke (13).

It was Blumenfeld who succeeded in persuading Albert Einstein to support the aims of the Zionists (14: aboard the S.S. "Rotterdam" on a voyage to America in 1921, with Ben Zion Mossinson, Chajim Weizmann, and Menachem Mendel Ussishkin).

German Zionists — Bearers Of A New Idea

Assimilation — An Illusion?

A dedicated journalist, Moritz Goldstein (1: with his wife at a Belgian sea resort, 1912) created a considerable stir with his essay "Deutsch-Juedischer Parnassus," which appeared in the magazine "Der Kunstwart" (2) in March 1912.

Goldstein pointed out as illusory the hope, wide-spread among the Jewish citizenry, that total social equality of the Jews was only a question of time.

"We Jews are caretakers of the spiritual sources of a people who deny us the right and the ability to that function.... For eight hundred years, ever since the Crusades, the Jews have been persecuted, slaughtered, mocked and reviled; why? Because they were so stubborn as to remain Jews, although Christianity existed in the world."

The first Jewish periodicals appeared in Prussia after 1750; none of them lasted very long. One exception was the Hebrew monthly "Hame'assef" (The Collector), founded by Moses Mendelssohn in 1784, which was published until 1811.

The 19th century saw the appearance of many journals and magazines, mostly in German, with vastly different tendencies, ranging from reformist to scientific, from Orthodox to Zionist.

"Der Israelit" (4) appeared from 1860 as a weekly for Orthodox Judaism.

The "Berliner Vereinsbote" (6) appeared from 1895 to 1902.

"Im Deutschen Reich" (3) was published from 1895 to 1921 as a monthly of the "Central Organization of German Citizens of the Jewish Faith", founded in 1893 in Berlin for the "active protection of the political and social equality of German Jews." Its main purpose was to combat anti-Semitism and to defend the civil rights of Jews.

The "C-V.-Zeitung" (5) appeared weekly from 1922 to November 1938 as successor to "Im Deutschen Reich."

Department stores were superior to the traditional specialty stores because of the variety of merchandise and the stores' luxurious interiors (2: the rug department).

...To Elegant Department Stores

The proliferation of elegant department stores with decorative exhibition areas, wide selections of merchandise and low prices received new impetus from the Tietz and Wertheim families. The concept had come from the United States.

In 1882 Hermann Tietz (3) owned a dry goods shop in Gera. Twenty years later, his chain of department stores stretched across all of Germany (1: The Tietz department store on Alexanderplatz in Berlin).

Pictures Of A Family

From Catherine Hanf Noren's photo album of a Jewish Family, "The Camera of My Family," published by Alfred A. Knopf, New York 1973.
My family lived in Germany from 1720 to 1939. In 1939 my parents had to leave. I was born shortly before they emigrated.

1903: The family after moving to Duesseldorf. Grandmother is the third from the right

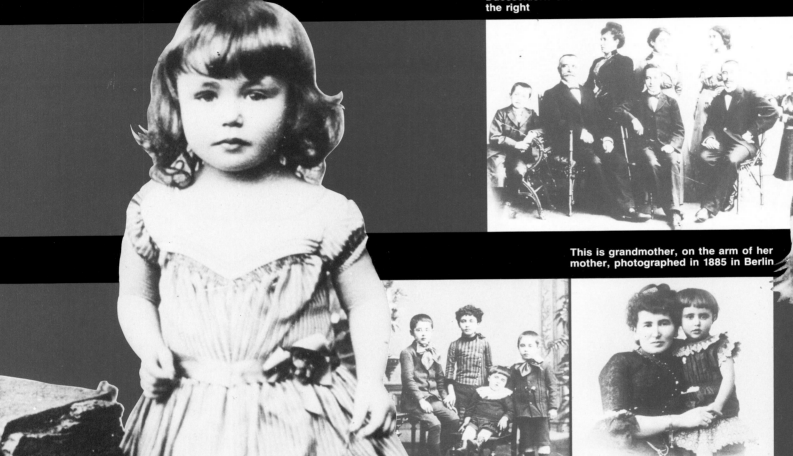

This is grandmother, on the arm of her mother, photographed in 1885 in Berlin

Grandmother's little sister, Grete, photographed on the arm of her nurse in 1893

Grandmother, seated, with her brothers and sisters. To the right her brother Oskar. He was killed by the Nazis

Grete and her husband, proud owners of an automobile, 1927

This is me, Catherine Hanf, in 1941 at the age of 3

Betty Wallach-Epstein, grandfather's sister with her husband and two daughters in 1925. She and her husband perished in a concentration camp

In 1908 Grandmother Meta fell in love with Moritz Wallach and got married the same year

My great-grandfather Samuel Strauss as a pensioner in his garden in Duesseldorf

Fritz — second from the right — as a soldier during the First World War

Three cousins — the youngest, Kaethe Mannheimer, was murdered with her husband in a concentration camp

Rolf was born in 1909. He was the first child of my grandparents

The Wallachs at the island of Wangeroog. One of the four children is my mother: Lotte, the third from the right

My mother, Lotte Hanf, with my sister Brigitte in 1938 just before I was born. One year later we fled Germany

Rolf was five years old when the First World War broke out

Rolf emigrated to the United States in 1928, at the age of 19. During the time of the Nazis, he rescued 10 members of the family Wallach — thirteen others were murdered by the Nazis

Erich Hanf, the man my mother fell in love with when she was sixteen years old. He later became my father

The following photos were taken in the textile factory Hanf & Kaufmann at Moenchen-Gladbach in 1938. My father was junior partner in the company

A tidy office

The Department of Design and Samples

Textile factory Hanf & Kaufmann: the factory wing

"Dangerous Activities"

The anti-Socialist legislation (1), in force from 1878 to 1890, allowed the police to harass members of the Social Democratic Party (4).
Paul Singer (3), a manufacturer, who had joined the party after the passage of the law, was expelled from Prussia in 1886 (2). He was allowed to return in 1887; in 1890, he joined the Executive Committee of the Social Democratic Party.

Their defence of the rights of the oppressed turned the Social Democrats into foes of any kind of discrimination. They perceived anti-Semitism to be an integral component of capitalist society. The question of how to fight effectively against it was the subject of many international congresses. It came up during the Congress of the Second International in Zurich, 1893 (5, from left to right: Dr. Simon, Frieda Simon, Clara Zetkin, Friedrich Engels, Julie Bebel, August Bebel, Ernst Schaffer, Regina Bernstein, Eduard Bernstein); and at the Congress of the Socialist International in Stuttgart, 1907, attended by Georg Ledebour, Karl Liebknecht, Julia Liebknecht, Leon Trotzky, Rosa Luxemburg, among others (6).

The social question was the key problem of German industrial society and its solution became the concern of many Jewish politicians, including Eduard Bernstein (7), a writer and member of the Reichstag; Hugo Haase (8), lawyer and member of the Weimar National Assembly; Hugo Preuss (9), political scientist, co-founder of the German Democratic Party in 1918, and Minister of the Interior, who played a leading role in drafting the Weimar Constitution; Paul Hirsch (10), Prussian Prime Minister and member of the Prussian Parliament; and Rosa Luxemburg (11), writer and politician.

"The vast majority of Jewish Social Democrats... believed, in accordance with their party's platform, that the victory of socialism would mean the solution of the Jewish question because 'it would result in the complete absorption' of the Jews."

Of the 26 Jewish deputies who sat in the Reichstag between 1893 and 1918, 17 were Social Democrats, 4 were left liberals, 4 were members of the National Liberal Party, and one belonged to a conservative faction.

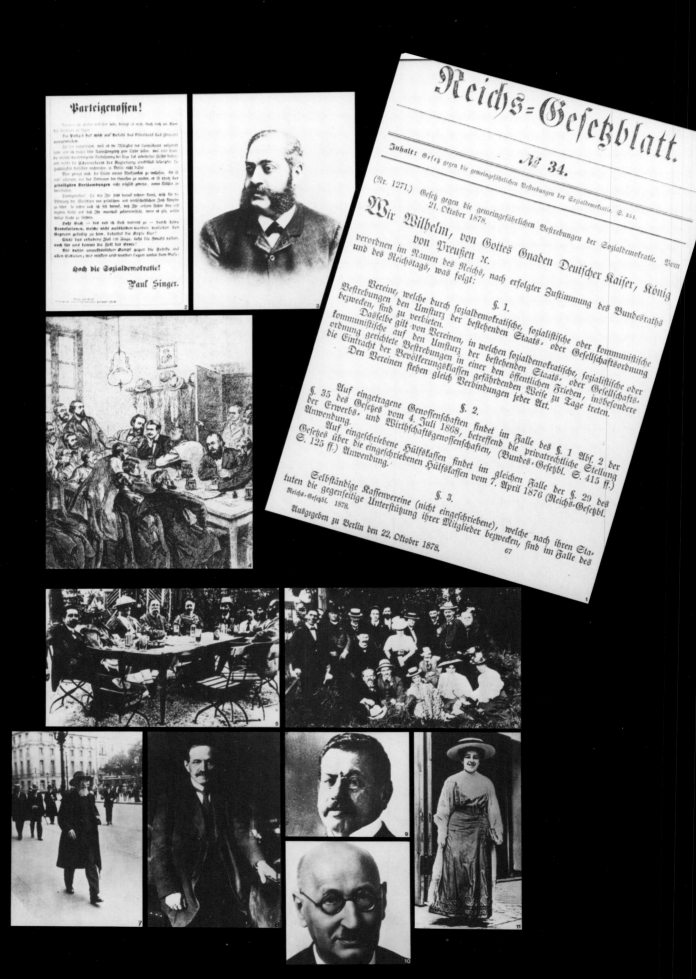

Emil Rathenau And The AEG — A Success Story

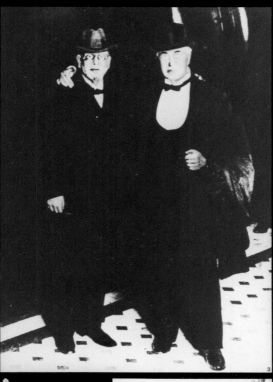

Emil Rathenau (1) had seen Edison's carbon filament lamp in Paris in 1881 and decided to acquire the patents. Two years later he founded the German Edison Company in Berlin which was renamed General Electricity Company (AEG) in 1887. Felix Deutsch (2) was Rathenau's right-hand man on the Board of Directors and his closest confidant.

The Ackerstrasse factory complex (4) was built in 1889, the Brunnenstrasse plant with the entrance for "white-collar employees" (6) in 1896.

In 1911, Thomas Alva Edison paid Rathenau a visit at the Moabit power station (3).

Rathenau's funeral cortege (Berlin, 1915) stretched for miles (5).

Levin Arons (2; his wife Lea, 1) was a banker. He financed the first railway from Berlin to Potsdam (3). His grandson Leo became a physicist and married Johanna Bleichroeder (4, 6). Appointed lecturer at the University of Berlin from 1889 onwards, he developed various methods of measuring physical processes.

In 1892 he invented the Arons' Oscillation Tube and a mercury vapour lamp (5).

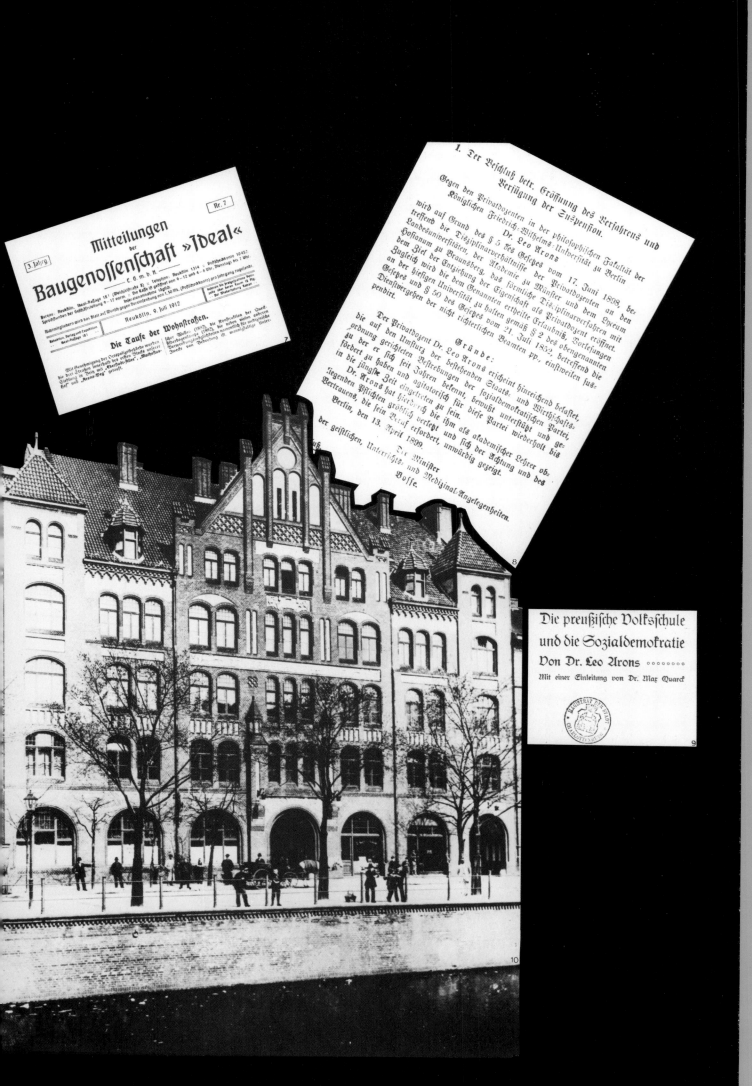

In 1898 he founded and financed 50% of the commercial enterprise Gewerkschaftshaus-GmbH in Berlin which opened in 1900 (10).

In 1899 he was dismissed from the university because he belonged to the SPD (German Socialist Party); the dismissal was based on a newly-promulgated law, the "Lex Arons" (8).

In 1905 Arons drafted a programme for a comprehensive primary school system in Prussia (9).

In 1912 a street in Berlin was named after him as co-founder and financial banker of the first co-operative workers' housing-project "Ideal" (7).

Several consumer and producer cooperatives owe their existence to his initiative.

"To Be What One Is"

The anti-Semitic ideology had spread through the German universities since the 1880's. Jewish students, banned from joining the regular student organizations, founded their own movements (4,5) as defence against anti-Semitism (6: Martin Buber, third from left in third row). As far as student traditions went, however, (dress, fencing, social life, etc.) they hardly differed from other organizations.

In a memorandum of the first Jewish student organization, the 'Viadrina' (2) founded in Breslau in 1886, we read:

"We take the position that we are Jews and can, at the same time, be Germans in the truest sense of the word. We want to make ourselves into men who will undertake whatever the state demands of its citizens with loyalty and enthusiasm...."

Their motto was: "To be what one is."

Many of these organizations were dominated by the idea of self-assertion (3). Others, for example, "Young Israel" (1), founded in 1891 in Berlin by Heinrich Loewe, and the student federation 'Maccabaea' (7; Felix Rosenblueth = Pinchas Rosen in centre) stood for Jewish national ideas.

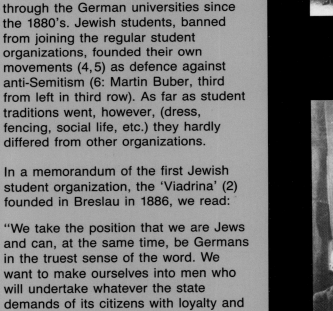

"The Jewish Problem — A Political Problem"

Die ägyptische Königstochter Rosa findet den Dr. Moses. So erklärt sich ihre Neigung für und seine Abneigung gegen das Gebären.

"The Jewish problem was always a political problem for me" wrote the seventy year old Julius Moses (1) in 1938. Four years later he was deported to Theresienstadt where he died shortly thereafter.

Julius Moses was a physician in Berlin and Social Democratic spokesman for health affairs in the Reichstag from 1920 to 1932 (5: caricature from the "Vorwaerts" in 1926). He belonged to the Executive Committee of the SPD (6; left to right: Wilhelm Dittmann, Luise Zietz, Arthur Crispien, Julius Moses, Anna Nemitz).

As early as 1912 he pleaded for birth control and advised the working class, "... not to bear more children than [they] can reasonably expect to be able to feed and educate" and pleaded for the liberation of the female proletariat "from the enslavement by their wombs...."

His opponents Rosa Luxemburg (3) and Clara Zetkin (4) in August 1913 attacked him, calling his appeal "bourgeois quackery." The satirical publication "Kladderadatsch" found an explanation for that position (2).

Marcus Mosse (2) was a physician. He had fourteen children: six daughters (3) and eight sons (4).

In 1868 his son Rudolf opened an advertising agency, the first of its kind in Germany. From the advertising business he moved into newspaper publishing.

The "Berliner Tageblatt" (1) first appeared in 1872 and soon reached a large circulation. After the First World War, the office building of the Mosse Publishing House (5) was considered one of the largest modern office facilities in Germany.

Bernhard Wolff — The Ullsteins

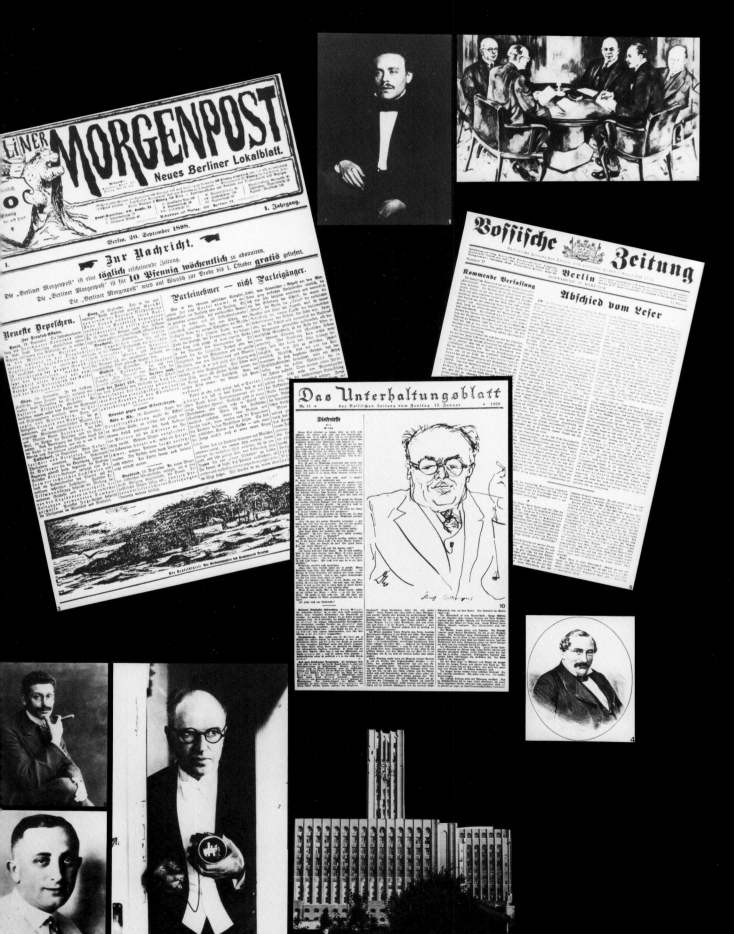

Journalism was one of the fields in which Jews were strongly represented.

In the year of the 1848 Revolution, Bernhard Wolff (4), a physician and journalist, established the Bureau for Telegraphic Correspondence B.W., later Wolff's Telegraph Bureau (W.T.B), Germany's first news agency.

Leopold Ullstein (1) founded a publishing house and acquired the "Berliner Illustrirte Zeitung" in 1894. His five sons (2: the "brothers' conference," from left to right: Hans, Franz, Louis Ferdinand, Rudolf, and Hermann) founded the "Berliner Morgenpost" (3) in 1898. Georg Bernhard (6) directed from 1908 until his dismissal in 1930 all Ullstein newspapers, and in 1914 he assumed the chief editorship of the prestigious "Vossische Zeitung" (5).

Egon Jacobsohn (7), who later changed his name to Jameson, was a reporter and editor; Erich Salomon (8) was a photo journalist; Paul Schlesinger (10) wrote his famous court reports under the pseudonym "Sling." The new Ullstein building in Berlin-Tempelhof (9) was erected in 1925/26.

A total of 147 dailies and weeklies appeared in Berlin in 1928.

Philosophers.........

.........Scientists

Actors

86 famous German stage and film actors took part in the memorial performance for the well-known actor Albert Steinrueck (4); 20 of them were banned and persecuted a few years later because of their Jewish ancestry.

1 Kurt Gerron
2 Gisela Werbezirk
3 Max Hansen
4 Albert Steinrueck commemoration on March 28, 1929
5 Alexander Granach
6 Paul Graetz
7 Grete Mosheim
8 Otto Wallburg
9 Eleonore von Mendelssohn
10 Fritz Gruenbaum
11 Hermann Vallentin
12 Conrad Veidt
13 Lucie Mannheim
14 Carola Neher
15 Ernst Deutsch
16 Max Pallenberg
17 Julius Falkenstein
18 Rosa Valetti
19 Fritzi Massary
20 Elisabeth Bergner
21 Fritz Kortner

Kurt Gerron, Otto Wallburg, and Fritz Gruenbaum were murdered in Auschwitz

Musicians..... Artists..... Architects

It would be a hopeless task to enumerate and assess the Jewish contribution to cultural life prior to 1933.

The potential loss by the madness of racism can best be perceived by asking the question, why Germany's former importance in the areas of science and art had been disrupted."

1 Felix Mendelssohn Bartholdy (1809-1847)
2 Autograph of the "Abendlied" by Mendelssohn Bartholdy
3 Copy of J. S. Bach's "St. Matthew's Passion" which was rediscovered by Felix Mendelssohn Bartholdy
4 Hugo Bock (1848-1932), owner of the music-publishing house of Bote & Bock, founded by his father in 1838
5 Entrance of the publishing house in Leipziger Strasse
6 Joseph Joachim (1831-1907), violinist. In 1868 he was appointed director of the Academy of Music in Berlin
7 Siegfried Ochs (1858-1929), founder and director of the Philharmonic Chorus
8 Andreas Weissgerber (1901-1942), violinist, emigrated in 1934 (drawing by Ludwig Meidner)
9 Otto Klemperer (1885-1973), conductor and composer, together with Igor Stravinsky (left) in Berlin in 1928
10 Victor Hollaender (1866-1940 died in exile), composer
11 Leo Blech (1871-1958), conductor
12 Bruno Walter (1876-1962), conductor
13 Friedrich Hollaender (1896-1976), composer, emigrated in 1933. Many of his songs were made popular by Marlene Dietrich
14 Max Liebermann (1847-1935), self portrait
15 Max Liebermann in his studio; photograph taken around 1900
16 Max Liebermann: "Flachsscheuer in Laren"
17 Guard of honour at the coffin of Max Liebermann on February 8, 1935 in the mourning hall of the Jewish cemetery on Schoenhauser Allee. Although it was forbidden by the Nazis, a Jewish photographer took his picture. In other times Liebermann would have received a state funeral
18 Ephraim Moshe Lilien (1874-1925), self portrait
19 Heinrich Tischler (1892-1938), self portrait
20 Lesser Ury (1861-1931), self portrait
21 Emil Orlik (1870-1932), photo
22 Joseph Budko (1888-1940), self portrait
23 Moritz Daniel Oppenheim (1800-1882), self portrait
24 Hermann Struck (1876-1944), lithograph by Joseph Budko

The architect Erich Mendelsohn (1887-1953) (1) was a member of the Prussian Academy of Arts. In 1920 he constructed the "Einsteinturm" (Einstein Tower) near Potsdam (3). His cinema at the Lehniner Platz in Berlin (2) was rebuilt as a theatre in 1980-81. Mendelsohn emigrated in 1933.

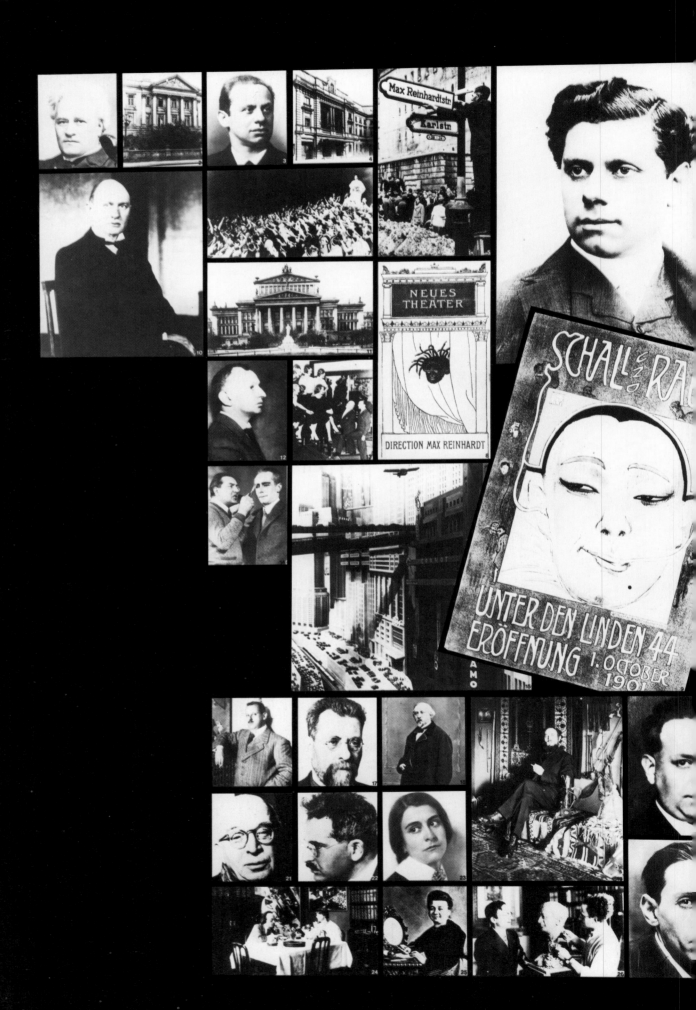

1 Ludwig Barnay (1842-1924), theatre director and actor, established the "Deutsches Theater" in 1882 and the "Berliner Theater" (2) in 1888; in 1899 he became director of the "Koenigliches Schauspielhaus", the Prussian Royal Theatre in Berlin

3 Otto Brahm (1856-1912), literary historian, critic, and stage manager. In 1892 he founded together with Paul Schlenther, Maximilian Harden, and Theodor Wolff the "Freie Buehne"; in 1894 he assumed the directorship of the "Deutsches Theater" (4)

6 Max Reinhardt (1873-1943), actor, theatre manager, director. In 1901 he co-founded the cabaret "Schall und Rauch" (9); in 1903 he took over the "Neues Theater" (8), and in 1905 the "Deutsches Theater" (4). In 1910: Performance of "Oedipus Rex" at the Schumann Circus (7). In 1920 Reinhardt co-founded the Salzburg Festival. He left for Austria in 1933 and emigrated to the USA in 1938.
On June 16, 1946, the Karlstrasse in Berlin was renamed Max-Reinhardt-strasse (5)

10 Leopold Jessner (1878-1945), theatre director at Koenigsberg. In 1918 he accepted the directorship of the Prussian State Theatre (11). Emigrated in 1935 to the USA

12 Felix Hollaender (1867-1931), author, and stage director at the "Deutsches Theater" from 1908-1913

13 Rudolf Nelson (1878-1960), pianist and composer of musical shows. Emigrated in 1933

16 Georg Hermann (1871-1943, murdered in Auschwitz), author

17 Julius Bab (1880-1955, died in exile), author and theatre critic

18 David Kalisch (1820-1872), author

19 Alfred Kerr (1867-1948), author and theatre critic; emigrated in 1933

20 Kurt Tucholsky (1890-1935, suicide in Sweden), author

21 Arnold Zweig (1887-1968), author; emigrated to Palestine in 1933, returned to East Germany

22 Walter Benjamin (1892-1940, suicide in Port Bou, France), literary theorist and writer

23 Else Lasker-Schueler (1869-1945, died in Jerusalem), poetess; emigrated in 1933

24 Herwarth Walden (1878-1943), art critic, moved to the Soviet Union in 1932

25 Friederike Kempner (1838-1904), poetess

26 Alfred Doeblin (1878-1957, physician and novelist, emigrated in 1933, returned to West Germany

27 Walter Mehring (1896-1981), author; emigrated in 1933

Fritz Lang (1890-1976) was film director
(see left page with Alfred Abel (14)
during the production of the film
''Metropolis'' (15) in 1925-26).

In 1923 he produced ''Die Nibelungen''
(First Part, UFA-Film) with Hanna Ralph
as Brunhild

The Great War and the Weimar Republic

Like their non-Jewish countrymen at the beginning of World War I, the majority of German Jews was swept along by enthusiastic patriotism. They hoped that the last barriers to complete emancipation could be overcome. Many Jewish volunteers heeded the call of Jewish organizations to give themselves completely in their services to the fatherland. These hopes, however, were not fulfilled. Anti-Semitic groups accused Jewish citizens of war-profiteering and of evading military service. In 1916 a *Jewish Census* was taken by the Prussian Ministry of War to assess the extent of Jewish military participation. The results, however, were never published. According to data compiled in 1932 by the National League of Jewish War Veterans, the share of Jewish soldiers, officers, medal winners, and casualties exactly matched that of non-Jews. Nevertheless, the legend of the Jewish draft dodger was never contradicted by the authorities.

After the November Revolution in 1918, anti-Semitism became even more acute. Demands for pogroms and the murder of Jews were openly voiced. Jews were accused of enriching their coffers through the misery of the German people, of causing the loss of the war, and of having brought about the November Revolution. The radical right wing propagandists began to equate Communism and Bolshevism with international Jewry. During this time, anti-Semitic publications defamed the Jews and held them responsible for all political misfortune. Thus, by fanning anti-Jewish hysteria, a climate was created which the National Socialists could utilize to further their aims.

The *basic rights statute* in the Weimar Constitution opened all state offices *de jure* to Jewish citizens. Walther Rathenau (1867-1922), for instance, became the first Jewish Minister of Foreign Affairs. His position exemplifies the ambiguous situation of Jewish citizens in the Weimar Republic: high public offices were open to them, yet the threat of militant anti-Semitism continued to grow. Rathenau's murder by right-wing nationalists underscored the precariousness of Jews in the Republic.

Religion was of little concern to Jews who participated in public life as politicians, artists, journalists, merchants, or scientists. Yet, when they defended themselves against anti-Semitic accusations, they acted as Jews. Many Jewish organizations co-operated: educational meetings were arranged, pamphlets distributed and defensive organizations established to protect Jewish citizens from encroachments upon their rights. German Jewry, in response to anti-Semitic accusations, always pointed out that they belonged much more to Germany and German culture than to Judaism.

The demand that Jews should abandon their identity as Jews in order to be accepted by German society had been nearly realized by the end of the Weimar Republic. Most Jewish citizens considered their religion a private matter. Germany was their homeland, and they lived as Germans in Germany.

Classification according to profession of the total population and of the Jewish population as of June 16, 1925

Total population:

- Without occupation or no profession given
- Domestic work
- Health care
- Self-employed
- Public administration
- Trade, commerce, gastronomy
- Agriculture, gardening, animal breeding, forestry and fishing
- Industry and handicraft including mining and building industry

Jewish population:

- Without profession or no profession given
- Domestic work
- Health care
- Self-employed
- Public administration
- Trade, commerce, gastronomy
- Agriculture, gardening, animal breeding, forestry, and fishing
- Industry and handicraft including mining and building industry

Distribution of professions among the Jewish population of Prussia

1861
- Without occupation or no profession given
- Domestic work and wage labour of varying classifications
- Commerce
- Self-employed, civil servants
- Agriculture
- Industry and handicraft
- Trade and banking

1907
- Without occupation or no profession given
- Domestic work and wage labour of varying classifications
- Commerce
- Self-employed, civil servants
- Agriculture
- Industry and handicraft
- Trade and banking

1925
- Without occupation or no profession given
- Domestic work and wage labour of varying classifications
- Commerce
- Self-employed, civil servants
- Agriculture
- Industry and handicraft
- Trade and banking

"Let The Sword Decide..."

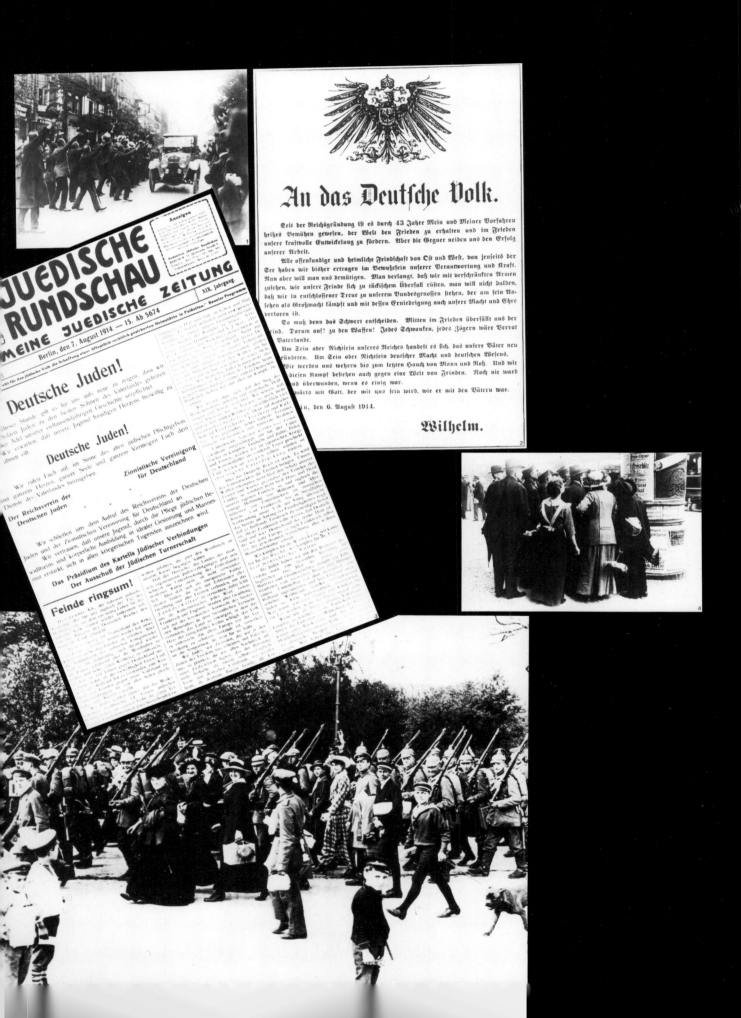

When Emperor William II travelled through the streets of Berlin on August 1, 1914 (1), and a few days later issued a "call to arms" to the German people (2), patriotism motivated the Jews of Prussia to express their loyalty.

All Jewish papers joined in the call (3). People crowded around the advertising posts to read the proclamations of the first days of war (4). Many Jewish volunteers were among the first soldiers who marched to the front (5), just as they did in 1813 and 1870: "I went to war as a German to protect my beleaguered fatherland; but I also went as a Jew in order to fight for the unconditional equality of my fellow Jews." (A soldier, 1914)

"Whoever Among You Dies In Battle, Dies for Me...."

Participation in the war offered German Jews the opportunity to demonstrate their patriotism; they thereby hoped to achieve complete social equality and recognition.

But by 1916 it once again became clear that all such hopes were an illusion. The rightist parties in Germany had succeeded in carrying the anti-Semitic mood as high as the Ministry of Defence; in October 1916, a "Jewish census" was ordered by edict. The "census" asked such questions as how many Jews had died in battle and how many had received the Iron Cross? Significantly, the results were never released during the war.

"General opinion held that we were aliens, that we stood aside, that we had to be treated as individual statistics, that we had to be counted, registered and handled separately. The dream of the community had ended; with one terrible blow the deep, eternal chasm once again opened before us."
(Ernst Simon)

1 Wilhelm Frankl, fighter pilot, Lieutenant in the Reserves
2 World War I volunteer Lichtenstein on leave
3 Jewish Knights of the Iron Cross First Class
4 Jewish soldiers of the 455th Infantry Regiment
5 "In the name of His Majesty the Emperor and King, the Iron Cross Second Class has been bestowed on...."
6 Jewish religious service in Brussels
7 Kurt Tucholsky (left)
8 Magnus Teitelbaum, reservist in Posen (later perished in a concentration camp)
9 Walter Sielmann (right), artillery officer in the Champagne

"...On The Field Of Honour...."

1914 IM WELTKRIEG 1916
starben aus unserer Gemeinde fürs Vaterland

DEINE TOTEN WERDEN LEBEN. Jes. 26, 19.

Siegfried Baruch
Artur Bernhardt
Theodor Bernstein
Eduard Blumenthal
Julius Bogusch
Carl Cohn
Curt Cohn
Justus Cohn
Victor Cohn
Siegfried Czarlinski
Erich Deutschland
Adolf Dubinski
Sally Feibel
Erich Flater
Max Gabrielski
Hans Ginsberg
Julius Glückauf
Bruno Goldstein
Siegfried Goldstein
Philipp Haushalter
Fritz Harnel
Adolf Hirschfeld
Bruno Heymann
Hugo Heymann
Wilhelm Heymann
Erich Jacoby
Willy Kaliski
Eduard Cohn

Benno Kendziorek
Siegfried Landau
Manfred Laufer
Heinrich Lehmann
Fritz Liepmann
Max Lindenbaum
Egon Löwinsohn
Julius Markus
Walter Marcuse
Siegfr. Maschkowski
Julius Meyer
Willy Meyer
David Pommer
Oskar Rabow
Ernst Rosenbaum
Hermann Rosenbaum
Leo Rosenbaum
Walter Rosenthal
Fritz Schlesinger
Adolf Schwarz
Philipp Schwersenz
Artur Sielmann
Gustav Stein
Fritz Sternberg
Willy Tuchler
Nathan Winterfeld
Georg Wolff
Louis Wolffberg

About	100,000	German Jews fought in the First World War
About	80,000	saw service at the front
About	35,000	were decorated
About	23,000	received promotions
About	12,000	gave their lives for their country

"...Born As A Second-Class Citizen."

> "Every German Jew experiences one painful moment in his youth which he remembers all his life: that moment when he first becomes fully conscious of the fact that he was born as a second-class citizen, and that no achievement or merit can liberate him from that condition. The ideas which form the basis of Prussia's policy regarding the Jews are obsolete, false, inexpedient and immoral."
> (Walther Rathenau)

Walther Rathenau (1), son of the founder of the AEG, became chairman of the board of this giant electrical company after his father's death. With the outbreak of the First World War, he played an active role in organizing the German war economy. In 1921 he served as Minister for Reconstruction, and in 1922 was named Minister of Foreign Affairs.

Four months later he was assassinated by members of the radical right (2), shortly after leaving his Koenigsallee villa (3) in the Berlin suburb of Grunewald (4). A protest demonstration of Berliners in front of the former Royal Palace on June 28, 1922 (5) was as impressive as it was unproductive.

Anti-Semitism —
A Current Of The Twenties

Anti-Semitism (1) had firm roots in the ideology of the nationalist and anti-democratic organizations and political parties since the beginning of the twentieth century. It assumed a central position in the platform of the National Socialist party from its inception.

The NS-propagandists Joseph Goebbels (2) and Julius Streicher (5) succeeded in mobilizing and manipulating the masses with slogans (3, 4) borrowed from figures as different as Martin Luther and the 19th century historian Heinrich von Treitschke.

The "Deutschnationale Volkspartei" (German National People's Party) began its election campaign in 1919 with anti-Semitic leaflets (6), in which even Clara Zetkin and Carl Kautsky were falsely identified as Jews. In 1932, the party fought its campaign "With God for Emperor and Fatherland" (7: at the rostrum, the party's national youth leader, and former district magistrate, Herbert von Bismarck). In June 1933 the party was dissolved.

"...Protect Yourself From This Poisonous Brood!"

Post-war anti-Semitic propaganda repeatedly accused the Jews of having shirked their military duty.

Jewish organizations actively challenged this lie as well as other accusations in leaflets and pamphlets (1-5) which were widely circulated from 1919 to 1932.

"The whole Jewish counterattack was targeted at one overriding goal: defending equal rights for Jews and the German Republic which guaranteed them."

German And Jewish Consciousness

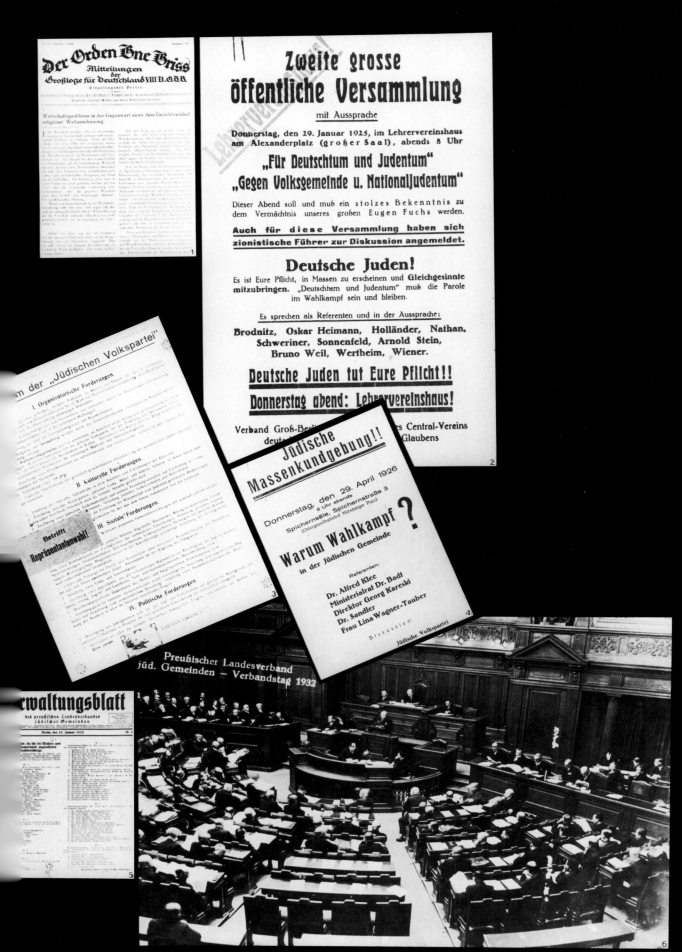

Many Jewish organizations and political parties became involved with matters concerning international as well as Jewish communal politics after 1918. Their goals were varied:

B'nai B'rith (1), literally "Sons of the Covenant," was an independent, apolitical and supranational order founded in New York in 1843 and in Berlin in 1882 for the "advancement of charity, humanity and friendship." From 1924 on, Leo Baeck was Grand Master of the "District of Germany" which had 103 lodges — not related to the Freemason lodges. The organization had 15,000 members.

The "Central Organization of German Citizens of the Jewish Faith," founded in 1893, tried to achieve a synthesis of German and Jewish consciousness during the Weimar Republic (2). With its principle of "maintaining the German spirit and sentiment," it represented the overwhelming majority of German Jews, thus placing itself in opposition to Zionism and the nationalist Jewish views of the "Juedische Volkspartei" (Jewish People's Party), founded in 1919 (3, 4).

The Prussian Association of Jewish Communities (5, 6) was created in Berlin in 1922 to represent the interests of some 700 Jewish communities throughout Prussia. It functioned until 1938.

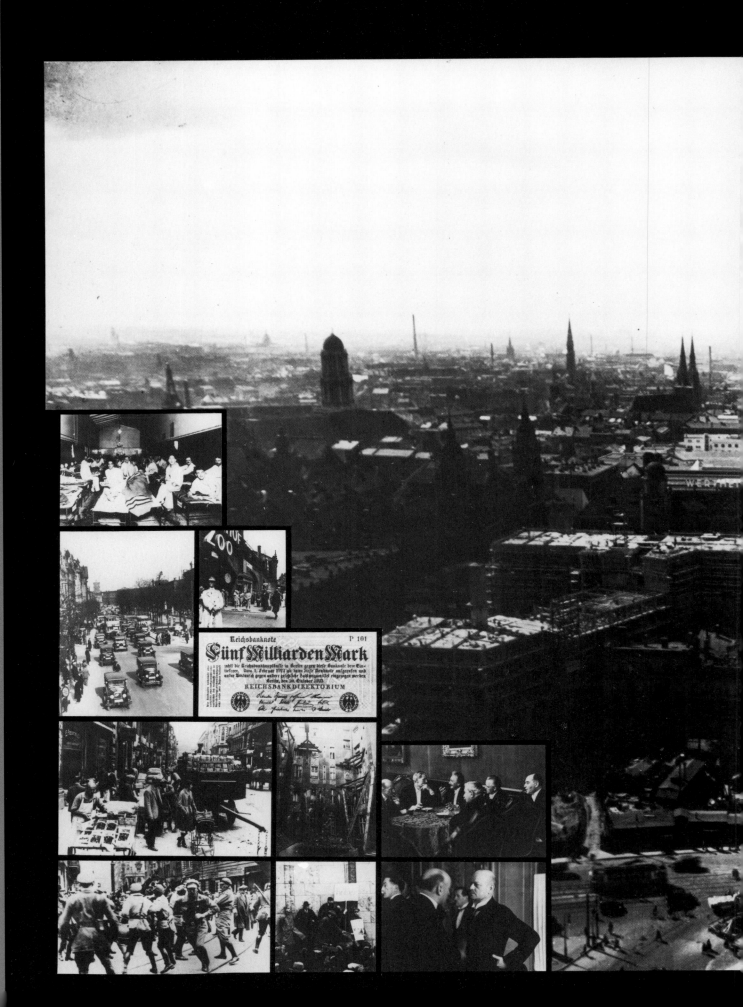

The prosperous stratum of the Jewish middle class were mainly entrepreneurs, merchants, physicians, lawyers, and other professionals. The middle stratum consisted of independent tradesmen and storekeepers, for example those in the garment businesses located near Hausvogteiplatz (1). The petty bourgeoisie was made up of tradesmen and craftsmen, many of whom could be seen around the Alexanderplatz (2), as well as white-collar workers.

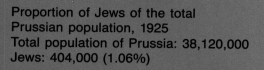

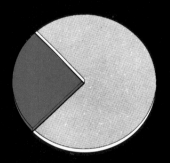

Proportion of Jews of the total
Prussian population, 1925
Total population of Prussia: 38,120,000
Jews: 404,000 (1.06%)

Proportion of Jews of the population
of Berlin, 1925
Total number of inhabitants: 4,100,000
Jews: 173,000 (4.3%)

Proportion of Eastern European Jews
of the total population of Berlin, 1925
Total number of Jews: 173,000
Eastern European Jews: 43,000 (25.4%)

Berlin radiated energy. It was a magnet
that attracted everyone, especially Jews
from Eastern Europe. They settled on a
few narrow streets, particularly Grenadier-
strasse (1-7), in the "Scheunenviertel,"
a densely populated slum neighbourhood
near Alexanderplatz. Their social
structure, traditional dress and way of
life set them apart from the remaining
assimilated Jewish population.

Welfare And Social Work

Lina Morgenstern (1) was a pioneer in modern social work and education. In 1859 she organized the first Froebel kindergartens which were based on the ideas of Friedrich Froebel (1782-1852), and had been prohibited in Prussia from 1851 to 1860 as "atheistic and socialistic." In 1866 she established Berlin's public soup kitchens and in 1869 an association for the protection of children and the first organization for the education of working women.

In 1892 Hermann Abraham (2) founded an association for the distribution of food for children (3, 4) and care centres in Berlin.

James Simon (5), a businessman, was a benefactor of Berlin museums. In the late 19th century he endowed Berlin's first communal swimming pools and supported child welfare and adult education; in 1901 he co-founded the "Hilfsverein der deutschen Juden," a relief organization aiding Jewish emigrants from Eastern Europe.

Alice Bendix (6) pioneered in childcare; she was director of a juvenile home in Berlin-Charlottenburg until 1933. In 1943 she was murdered in Auschwitz.

Alice Salomon (7) was an educator, founder and director of the first German school for social work for women, and a leading member of the Jewish women's movement. In 1937 she was expelled from Germany.

Hannah Karminski (9, 10), also an educator in the field of social work, was business manager of the "Juedischer Frauenbund" (League of Jewish Women). She was deported in 1942.

A class of the municipal Jewish grammar school (8) in Essen, 1922.

Social Welfare And Education

1   Day room in the Jewish Home for the Aged, Iranische Strasse, Berlin, 1934/35
2   A woman's bedroom at the same facility, 1934/35
3   Old Age Home, Berlin-Koepenick
4   School class picture, 1923
5   Jewish Home for the Aged, Landsberg/Warthe, 1920
6   Workers settlement of the Jewish Community, Berlin-Weissensee
7   Jewish Institute for the Deaf, Berlin-Weissensee

"Unity Brings Strength — Education Brings Freedom"

"I actually see it as a woman's mission to exercise every possible influence in the field of education so that the vain principles of honour, glory, and nationalism will be eradicated in the next generation," wrote the feminist Fanny Lewald (1) in one of her letters to Karl Alexander, Grand Duke of Saxe-Weimar, in January 1868.

When freedom of trade and commerce was legalized one year later, she demanded that the same freedoms be granted to all women because they had equal rights to continued education and independence.

In 1904, Berta Pappenheim (2) founded the "Juedischer Frauenbund," (League of Jewish Women) devoting herself to caring for the needy and homeless and fighting against white slave trade.

One generation later, the social scientist Cora Berliner (4) began defending women's rights. She became an adviser to the "Reichsvertretung der deutschen Juden," a Nazi-imposed organization of all Jews in Germany. She was deported in 1942.

Anti-abortion-law demonstration (3), Leipzig, 1928.

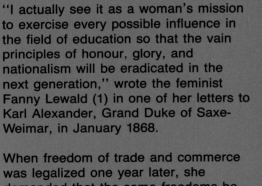

Die Arbeiterin

Heraus mit dem Frauenwahlrecht

FRAUEN-TAG
8. MÄRZ 1914

Den Frauen, die als Arbeiterinnen, Mütter und Gemeindebürgerinnen ihre volle Pflicht erfüllen, die im Staat wie in der Gemeinde ihre Steuern entrichten müssen, hat Voreingenommenheit und reaktionäre Gesinnung das volle Staatsbürgerrecht bis jetzt verweigert.
Dieses natürliche Menschenrecht zu erkämpfen, muß der unerschütterliche, feste Wille jeder Frau, jeder Arbeiterin sein. Hier darf es kein Ruhen kein Rasten geben. Kommt daher alle, ihr Frauen und Mädchen in die am

Sonntag den 8. März 1914 nachmittags 3 Uhr stattfindenden

9 öffentl. Frauen-Versammlungen

Gymnastics, Track, Fencing...

At the fifth Zionist Congress, Basel, 1901, the physician, writer and politician Max Nordau stressed the importance of physical fitness for Jews.

The Berlin Jewish sports clubs Bar Kochba (1, 3) and Maccabi had more than 10,000 members in the 20's. Youngsters (4) and students (2) trained in the provinces as well.

In 1919 Ernst Simon became Brandenburg champion of the 800 metre race (5); Martel Jacob (6) was the German javelin throwing champion in 1929.

The Jewish community had its own athletics field in Berlin-Grunewald (7). Helene Mayer (8) became the Olympic fencing champion in 1928. Aviator Guenther von Huenefeld (9, on right), with Koehl and Fitzmaurice, was the first to fly across the Atlantic from East to West in April 1928.

In the Nazi-State: Deprivation of Rights, Expulsion, Mass-Murder

From the beginning of our century, anti-Semitism occupied a central position in the programmes of nationalistic and anti-democratic groups. The Nazi party made it the focal point of their political thought. The Nazis declared Capitalism as well as Communism to be *Jewish;* this formula enabled them to attack the Jew as the one common enemy in their social and political arguments. A systematic propaganda campaign stirred up prejudice and resentment against the Jews in broad sections of the population. This climate eventually allowed the Nazis to commit genocide without encountering appreciable resistance from the population.

After their seizure of power in January 1933, the National Socialists quickly moved to eliminate their political enemies. Brutal terror was used against the Communist Party, the Social Democratic Party and the Labour Unions. At the same time, the German Jews became the victims of increasingly repressive economic and social measures. Gradually, Jewish capital assets were *aryanized,* that is handed over to non-Jewish capitalists.

Numerous anti-Semitic laws and statutes systematically isolated Jewish citizens from non-Jews. The *Nuremberg laws* of September 15, 1935, legalized this Nazi barbarism.

Organizations such as the *"Reichsvertretung der Deutschen Juden"* (National Represen-tation of German Jews) assisted the Jews recently deprived of their rights by preparing their emigration and attempting to ease the living conditions for those who remained in Germany. They established a comprehensive Jewish school system as well as social work organizations, and welfare aid societies. Jewish artists were forced to work within the *"Kulturbund"* (Cultural Association of German Jews). These organizations operated under constantly worsening conditions and increasing outside pressure.

Denied all hope of a human way of life in their German homeland, more than half of the German-Jewish population emigrated. Those who remained were forced once again to wear the yellow star. The anti-Semites' and Hitler's threat to annihilate the Jewish people was finally carried out by the Nazis during the war years.

123,000 German Jews were murdered. A total of six millions Jews died in Europe as victims of the National Socialist terror. The concentration camps were situated in Germany and the annihilation camps in Poland.

The non-Jewish German population was either not willing or not able to stop this crime, or swore that they knew nothing whatsoever about it.

Selected Laws, Regulations, Actions of the National Socialist State

Legislation in 1869 had brought the Jews legal equality in Prussia and shortly thereafter throughout the German Empire. From 1933 on, Nazi laws and regulations gradually and systematically rescinded all these rights throughout Germany.

1933

April 1
Start of the boycott of businesses owned by German citizens of the Jewish faith and of Jewish descent.

April 7
Law for the Restoration of the Professional Civil Service:
§ 3 (1) *"Civil servants who are not of Aryan descent are to be retired ...."*
World War I veterans and their family members are exempt. The foremost purpose of this law is the dismissal of political opponents in the civil service.

May 10
Burning of books whose contents had been declared *un-German* by the Nazis.

September 22
Formation of the National Chamber of Culture and its suborganizations. Membership is obligatory for persons engaged in the cultural sector; Jews are excluded.

1934

Febrary 5 to December 8
New rules governing state examinations for physicians, lawyers, and pharmacists: *Non-aryans* are excluded from these examinations.

1935

July 25
Non-aryans are not permitted to serve in the armed forces.

September 15
The *Nuremberg Laws,* the *Reich Citizenship Law,* and the *Law for the Protection of German Blood and German Honour* legalize the Nazis' anti-Semitic policies.

Reich Citizenship Law

The Reichstag has unanimously enacted the following law which is herewith made public:

§ 1
(1) A subject of the State is anyone who enjoys the protection of the German Reich and who therefore is especially obligated to it.
(2) State citizenship is acquired in accordance with the provisions of the Reich and State Citizenship Law.

§ 2
(1) Only the State citizen of German or of kindred blood who by his conduct proves that he is willing and able to serve loyally the German people and the Reich is a Reich citizen.
(2) Reich citizenship is acquired through the granting of a Reich Citizenship Certificate.
(3) The Reich citizen is the sole bearer of full political rights in accordance with the Law.

§ 3
The Reich Minister of the Interior, in co-ordination with the Deputy of the Fuehrer, will issue the Legal and Administrative orders required to implement and complete this Law.

Nuremberg, September 15, 1935
at the Reich Party Congress of Freedom
The Fuehrer and Reich Chancellor
Adolf Hitler
The Reich Minister of the Interior
Frick

Law for the Protection of German Blood and German Honour

Moved by the understanding that purity of the German Blood is the essential condition for the continued existence of the German people, and inspired by the inflexible determination to ensure the existence of the German Nation for all time, the Reichstag has unanimously adopted the following Law, which is promulgated herewith:

§ 1
(1) Marriages between Jews and subjects of the State of German or related blood are forbidden. Marriages nevertheless concluded are invalid, even if concluded abroad to circumvent this Law.
(2) Annulment proceedings can be initiated only by the State Prosecutor.

§ 2
Extramarital intercourse between Jews and subjects of the State of German or related blood is forbidden.

§ 3
Jews may not employ in their households female subjects of the State of German or related blood who are under 45 years old.

§ 4
(1) Jews are forbidden to fly the Reich or National flag or to display the Reich colours.
(2) They are, on the other hand, permitted to display the Jewish colours. The exercise of this right is protected by the State.

§ 5
(1) Any person who violates the prohibition under § 1 will be punished by a prison sentence with hard labour.
(2) A male who violates the prohibition under § 2 will be punished with a prison sentence with or without hard labour.
(3) Any person violating the provisions under §§ 3 or 4 will be punished with a prison sentence of up to one year and a fine, or with one or the other of these penalties.

§ 6
The Reich Minister of the Interior, in co-ordination with the Deputy of the Fuehrer and the Reich Minister of Justice, will issue the Legal and Administrative regulations required to implement and complete this Law.

§ 7
The Law takes effect on the day following promulgations except for § 3, which goes in force on January 1, 1936.

Nuremberg, September 15, 1935
at the Reich Party Congress of Freedom
The Fuehrer and Reich Chancellor Adolf H
The Reich Minister of the Interior Frick
The Reich Minister of Justice Dr. Guertn
The Deputy of the Fuehrer R. Hess

November 14
First Regulation of the Reich Citizenship La
.....
§ 4
(1) A Jew cannot be a Reich citizen. He ha no voting rights in political matters; he can hold public office.
(2) Jewish civil servants will retire as of December 31, 1935 ....

§ 5
(1) A Jew is a person descended from at least three grandparents who are full Jews race ....
(2) Also to be considered a Jew is a partl Jewish national who is descended from tw fully Jewish grandparents and
a) who was a member of the Jewish Religious Community at the time of the promulgation of this Law, or was admitted subsequently;
b) who was married to a Jew at the time the promulgation of this Law, or subseque married to a Jew;
c) who was born from a marriage with a (as defined in § 5, 1) contracted subseque to the promulgation of the Law for the Protection of German Blood and German Honour of September 15, 1935 *(Reichsgesetzblatt,* I, p. 1146);
d) who was born as the result of extramar intercourse with a Jew in accordance with 5, 1) and was born illegitimately after July 1936 ....

37

ril 15
ws of German nationality are no longer
owed to receive doctorates.

38

25
ish physicians lose their licenses.

gust 17
cond Regulation for the implementation of
Law Concerning Alteration of Family
nes and First Names:

of January 1, 1939, Jews whose first
nes differ from those permitted under § 1
required to accept an additional name
ch will be Israel for males, Sara for
ales.

tember 27
ish lawyers lose their right to practise.

ober 5
marking of Jewish passports with the
er "J."

ober 27/28
ortation of Jews formerly or still holding
sh nationality from Germany to the
man-Polish border. The Polish government
lly prevented these Jews from entering
nd.

ember 9/10
e-organized pogrom, the so-called *Night
ne Broken Glass*. Arrest and murder of
ish citizens. Almost all synagogues in
many are devastated and burned, and
t Jewish stores are ransacked.

ember 12
e totality of Jews who are German
ects will pay a fine of one billion
hsmarks to the German Reich."
fine is explained as a "severe expiation"
he hostile attitude of Jewry toward the
man people.

ember 15
sh children are excluded from state
ols.

ember 3/6
s are not allowed to own or to drive cars,
ter theatres, cinemas, cabarets, public
erts, libraries, museums, public and
te swimming pools, and sports grounds.
dition, they are not permitted to enter the
rnment district in Berlin.
s can be ordered to sell their businesses,
they have to deposit their stocks and
ds in specified banks.

ember 8
are excluded from universities.

1939

February 21
Jews of German nationality must surrender all
items of gold, silver, and platinum, as well as
pearls and precious stones within two weeks
to state purchasing agencies. An exception
will be made for wedding rings only.

July 4
Establishment of the *Reichsvereinigung der
Juden in Deutschland* (National Representation
of German Jews). Membership is obligatory
for all Jews.

September 23
A police decree orders the surrender of radios
owned by Jews.

October 20
By order of the Minister of Education, German
scholars are required not to quote any Ph.D.
dissertations written by Jews. If scholarly
reason still demand the inclusion of such
material, the author has to be marked as
Jewish.

1940

February 10 to 12
First deportations to Poland from Stettin,
Stralsund, and Schneidemuehl.

July 4
Grocery shopping by Jews in Berlin is
restricted to one hour from 4 to 5 p.m.

1941

September 1
Police decree concerning identification of Jews:
§ 1
(1) *All Jews from the age of six are prohibited
from appearing in public without displaying the
Jewish star.*

October 10
Jews are forbidden to leave their homes
without police permission.

October 18
Start of deportations to Lodz, Minsk, Kowno,
Riga, Auschwitz, Trawniki, Tallinn, Lublin,
Ravensbrueck, Sachsenhausen, and Bergen-
Belsen.

November 17 and 27
Deportation of Berlin Jews to Kowno and
Riga. None survived; all were executed.

November 25
"Resettlement Action" of German Jews from
Berlin, Frankfurt/Main, and Munich to Kowno.

December 26
Jews are forbidden to use public telephones.

1942

January 10
Jews are ordered to surrender all furs and
woollen materials.

January 20
Excerpt from the protocol of the Wannsee
Conference concerning the *Final Solution of
the Jewish Question: As part of the Final
Solution Jews under appropriate control, are
to be utilized for work in the East in an
expedient manner. Jews who are physically fit
will be separated according to sex and taken
to the East in order to build roads. As a
result of this action, there is no doubt that a
majority of them will perish through natural
attrition.*

May 15
Jews are forbidden to keep pets.

June 6
The first of 117 deportations of elderly Jews
from Berlin to Theresienstadt. The last
deportation took place on March 27, 1945.

July 7
Jews are not allowed to enter waiting rooms
and restaurants and are forbidden to use
public transportations.

September 18
New shopping restrictions for Jews:
they no longer receive ration cards for meat,
clothing, milk, tobacco, white bread, and
merchandise in short supply.

1943

February 27
Deportation of Jewish workers employed in
Berlin armament factories to Auschwitz.

March 11
Decree of the *Reichssicherheitshauptamt*
(Reich Security Main Office):
*After completion of a prison term, Jews are to
be sent to the concentration camps at
Auschwitz or Lublin for the rest of their lives.*

June 10
Dissolution of the National Representation of
German Jews.

July 1
Jews lose all judicial protection and become
subject to police authority.

Number of Jews in Germany:

1933	525,000
1939	215,000
1941	164,000

Number of Jews in Berlin:

1933	160,600
1939	82,800
1942 January	55,000
1942 December	33,000
1943 April	18,300

There were a total of 63 "Osttransporte"
(transports to the East) claiming 35,000
victims and 117 "Altersstransporte"
(transports of the elderly) resulting in
15,000 victims.

A total of 123,000 German Jews perished.
Six millions Jews were victims of National
Socialist terror in Europe. Approximately
10,000 Jews survived the Third Reich in
Germany: of these 5,000 had been in
hiding; the remaining 5,000 were survivors
of concentration camps.

Closing ceremony of the Catholic Youth meeting on the athletics field, Berlin-Neukoelln, August 20, 1933

"So I believe to act in the spirit of the almighty God: By defending myself against the Jew I am fighting for the work of the Lord."
(Adolf Hitler in "Mein Kampf")

Der Führer: „So glaube ich im Sinne des allmächtigen Schöpfers zu handeln: Indem ich mich des Juden erwehre, kämpfe ich für das Werk des Herrn."

(„Mein Kampf", Seite 70)

"Every Person Must Submit
To The Supreme Authorities"

(Paul, Romans 13)

The Boykott

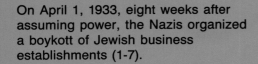

Jüdisches Geschäft! Wer hier kauft wird photographiert

On April 1, 1933, eight weeks after assuming power, the Nazis organized a boykott of Jewish business establishments (1-7).

Thereafter obligatory emigration was introduced. The estimated Jewish population in Germany in 1933: 525,000.

During the period from 1933 to the end of World War II, more than half the Jewish population emigrated, primarily to the following countries:

USA	132,000
Palestine	55,000
British Dominions	40,000
Argentina	20,000
Brazil	13,000
Shanghai	12,000

JÜDISCHE RUNDSCHAU

*Tragt ihn mit Stolz,
den gelben Fleck!*

Der JÜDISCHE KULTURBUND *arbeitet*

FÜR *Sie*!

Robert Weltsch, editor-in-chief of the "Juedische Rundschau," exhorted Jews in his proclamation on April 4, 1933, to "wear it with pride, the yellow badge" (1).

In response to the expulsion of Jewish artists from general cultural life, the "Kulturbund deutscher Juden" (German-Jewish Cultural Association) was founded in June 1933 (5). Nazi laws increasingly restricted the freedom of movement of Jews; soon, social contact was also only possible with other Jews.

2   Puppet show at the Alexandrinen-strasse Jewish kindergarten in Berlin, 1934
3   Meeting in the Prinzregentenstrasse synagogue, Berlin, 1935
    Two Gestapo agents, heads uncovered, are seated in the second from top row
4   Concert at the Oranienburgerstrasse synagogue, Berlin, 1938
11 Coffee at the Hirschfeld home, Berlin, 1939
12 Dress rehearsal of the Youth Orchestra of the Berlin Jewish Community, 1937
13 Fiftieth anniversary of the Schoen-hauser Allee Old Age Home in Berlin, with community leaders Heinrich Stahl, Moritz Rosenthal, and Rabbi Warschauer in the front row (left to right)

Some Jewish institutions were still tolerated for a time:

6   Ismar Elbogen lecturing at the "Hochschule (Lehranstalt) fuer die Wissenschaft des Judentums" (Institute for Jewish Studies), Berlin, 1935
7   Library of the Rabbinical Seminary, Berlin, 1935
8   Institute for Jewish Studies, 1936
9   Rabbinical Seminary, 1936
10 Martin Buber delivering a lecture on Chassidism in the hall of the Berlin Singakademie on January 17, 1935.

In The Hour Of Peril

In September 1933 Jewish organizations and Jewish communities united together and founded the "Reichsvertretung der deutschen Juden" (National Representation of German Jews) to negotiate with the Nazi authorities on behalf of all German Jews. Its president was Leo Baeck, the senior rabbi of Berlin.

Meeting of the presiding council (8), 1933. (left to right): Franz Meyer, Breslau; Rabbi Jacob Hoffmann, Frankfurt/Main; Siegfried Moses (10), Berlin; Rabbi Leo Baeck, standing; Otto Hirsch (7), Stuttgart, who was murdered in 1941 at the Mauthausen concentration camp; Rudolph Callmann, Cologne; Heinrich Stahl, Berlin, who perished in 1942 in Theresienstadt. Julius L. Seligsohn (9), another member of the presiding body, was murdered in 1942 at the Sachsenhausen concentration camp.

Paralleling the "Winter Relief Organization of the German People," which excluded Jews, the "Jewish Winter Relief" (2, 3) was established in 1933.

The systematic removal of Jews from their professions forced them to create self-help agencies: a central office for economic assistance was established in the Jewish community building on Rosenstrasse in Berlin (1, 4, 6), and the "Hilfsverein" of Jews in Germany opened an information office to advise and assist emigrants (5).

One Among Many

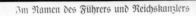

The merchant Hermann Simson was a descendant of Eduard von Simson, who in 1849 had presented the Imperial crown to Frederick William IV and, in 1871, to William I.

Hermann Simson participated in the First World War as reservist (2); was made staff sergeant in 1918 (3); received the Iron Cross in 1919 (4), the Combatant's Cross of Honour in 1935 (5) and, in 1944, was assigned the prisoner's number of 3,065 while a forced labourer (1).

Reich Citizenship Law

The Reichstag has unanimously enacted the following law which is herewith made public:

§ 1
(1) A subject of the State is anyone who enjoys the protection of the German Reich and who therefore is especially obligated to it.
(2) State citizenship is acquired in accordance with the provisions of the Reich and State Citizenship Law.

§ 2
(1) Only the State citizen of German or of kindred blood who by his conduct proves that he is willing and able to serve loyally the German people and the Reich is a Reich citizen.
(2) Reich citizenship is acquired through the granting of a Reich Citizenship Certificate.
(3) The Reich citizen is the sole bearer of full political rights in accordance with the Law.

§ 3
The Reich Minister of the Interior, in co-ordination with the Deputy of the Fuehrer, will issue the Legal and Administrative orders required to implement and complete this Law.

Nuremberg, September 15, 1935
at the Reich Party Congress of Freedom
    The Fuehrer and Reich Chancellor
        Adolf Hitler
    The Reich Minister of the Interior
        Frick

Law for the Protection of German Blood and German Honour

Moved by the understanding that purity of the German Blood is the essential condition for the continued existence of the German people, and inspired by the inflexible determination to ensure the existence of the German Nation for all time, the Reichstag has unanimously adopted the following Law, which is promulgated herewith:

§ 1
(1) Marriages between Jews and subjects of the State of German or related blood are forbidden. Marriages nevertheless concluded are invalid, even if concluded abroad to circumvent this Law.
(2) Annulment proceedings can be initiated only by the State Prosecutor.

On September 15, 1935, during the "National Party Assembly for Freedom" in Nuremberg, laws were issued which "separated the German people from the Jews", decreed the "racial inferiority" of the Jews and established guidelines for their exclusion from the German community.

"We, who are members of German youth movements, students, lawyers in German courts of law; we have become Jews by fiat. Gates have shut behind us, and we stand abandoned at the cross-roads." (Abraham Margaliot)

Rebuilding Amid Ruin

Kindertransport
Nr. 16
England

Compelled by Nazi terror many Jews had to consider emigration (8). The co-operation of all Jewish organizations made an intensive retraining programme for new jobs possible.

Crafts (1, 2, 4, 5) and agriculture (6: kibbutz-girl canvassing for aliya), were important areas of training. Special language courses were offered (3) and counselling offices (7) were established.

Calm Before The Storm — The Olympic Games Of 1936

The 100 meter runners (2, left to right: Levin, Schattmann, Gerson, Aufrichtig) trained for the Olympics on the athletics field of the Berlin Jewish community (1: boxes for the guests of honour).

It was Undersecretary Theodor Lewald (3), a lawyer of Jewish ancestry and Germany's representative in the International Olympic Committee, who succeeded in having Berlin selected as the site of the Olympics, which opened on August 1, 1936 (4).

Prior to the opening of the games, he reviewed the honour guard on Berlin's famed avenue, Unter den Linden, together with IOC president Count Baillet-Latour and the town major Lieutenant General Schaumburg (5).

Three women of Jewish ancestry won medals in the Olympic fencing competition. Gold: Ilona Elek-Schacherer (Hungary), Silver: Helene Mayer (right, Germany), Bronze: Ellen Preis (left, Austria) (6).

The November Pogrom

Ninety-one Jews were murdered during the pogrom on the night of November 9/10, 1938; some 280 synagogues and more than 7,000 Jewish business establishments were destroyed or badly damaged. The Nazis called the pogrom "Reichskristallnacht" (Night of the Broken Glass). 30,000 Jews were deported to concentration camps.

A decree of November 12, 1938 ordered the Jews to make an "atonement" payment of one billion Reichsmarks (i.e., $ 400,000,000) for the damages incurred. This sum was to be paid to the government within six weeks.

1, 2, 5   Fasanenstrasse synagogue in Berlin
3, 6   Jewish stores
4   Tora reading pulpit from the synagogue in Zeven, district of Bremervoerde

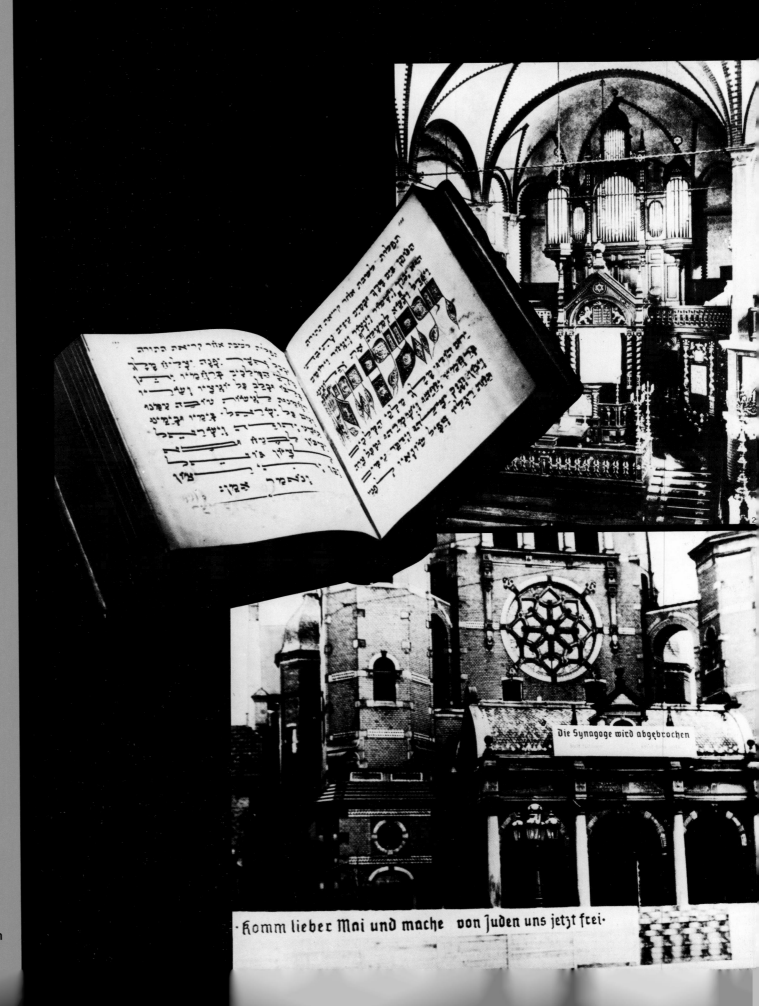

Danzig, a German city until 1919, became a Free City under the League of Nations. But when the Nazis won a majority in the Danzig parliament in 1935, persecution of the Jews and the violation of their civil rights followed. Danzig adopted the Nuremberg Laws in 1938. One year later, on June 9th, the Great Synagogue (2), built in 1887 and one of the most beautiful in Europe, was demolished (3). Valuable items from its interior (1) were rescued and shipped to New York.

Die Synagoge wird abgebrochen

Komm lieber Mai und mache   von Juden uns jetzt frei.

Defamation And Deportation

Wer dieses
Zeichen trägt,
ist ein
Feind
unseres Volkes

"Jews who have completed their sixth year are prohibited from appearing in public without displaying a Jewish star.

The Jewish star consists of a star with six points, the size of the palm of a hand, black on yellow, with the inscription 'Jew' in black. It is to be worn in full view, solidly fastened onto the left side of the outer garment."

(Police order concerning identification of Jews in Germany, September 1, 1941)

"Fuehrer, Command! We Will Follow You!"

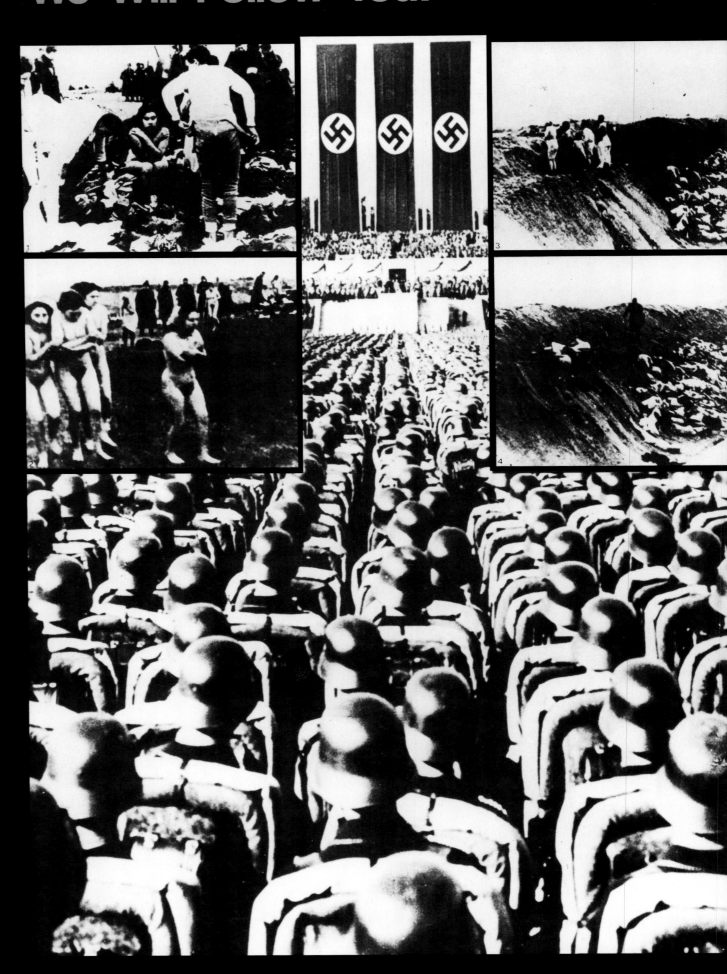

Action of the "Einsatzgruppen" (special task forces) in Liepaja, Latvia, on December 15, 1941, photographed by SS member Carl Sturm (1-4).

Lineup of SS units at the "National Party Assembly of Honour", Nuremberg, 1936 (5).

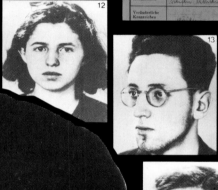

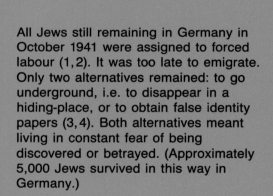

All Jews still remaining in Germany in October 1941 were assigned to forced labour (1,2). It was too late to emigrate. Only two alternatives remained: to go underground, i.e. to disappear in a hiding-place, or to obtain false identity papers (3,4). Both alternatives meant living in constant fear of being discovered or betrayed. (Approximately 5,000 Jews survived in this way in Germany.)

In 1940 some 500 Jewish forced labourers were assigned to the Berlin electrical motor factory of Siemens-Schuckert AG. Herbert Baum (6) was the leader of an anti-fascist resistance group consisting primarily of young Jews who printed and distributed pamphlets and leaflets.

When on May 18, 1942 twelve members of this group set fire to the National Socialist exhibition the "Soviet Paradise" shown in Berlin (5), almost all of the group's members were arrested (6-16), sentenced to death and executed.

MARSH USED FOR
ASH DISPOSAL

CONVOYS

CON

NE

AUSCHWITZ I

EXTERMINATION CAMP

SS BARRACKS AND HQ

SPUR

AUSCHWITZ-BIRKENAU COMPLEX
OSWIECIM, POLAND
26 JUNE 1944

The "Nuremberg Laws" of September 15, 1935 provided the legal basis for the discrimination of Jews.
These anti-Semitic policies led to the mass arrests of Jews after the November pogroms of 1938.

On September 1, 1939 Nazi Germany attacked Poland. This marked the beginning of World War II and the organized extermination of European Jewry.

Resettlement, evacuation, conscripted labour, special treatment — terms used veil organized deportation and murder

Police, SS, Wehrmacht (armed forces), and Reichsbahn (National Railways) participated in executing the terror of the Nazis

... is A Master From Germany" (From "Death Fugue by Paul Celan)

"In the course of the Final Solution of the European Jewish question approximately eleven million Jews may be taken into consideration .... They will be put to work in the East in appropriate ways." (From the Protocol of the Wannsee Conference January 20, 1942)

The newly established ghettos became waiting rooms on the road to the death camps

Helpless people mocked and tortured

In the spring of 1943, the Jews of the Warsaw Ghetto defended themselves five weeks against the militarily superior SS-Units

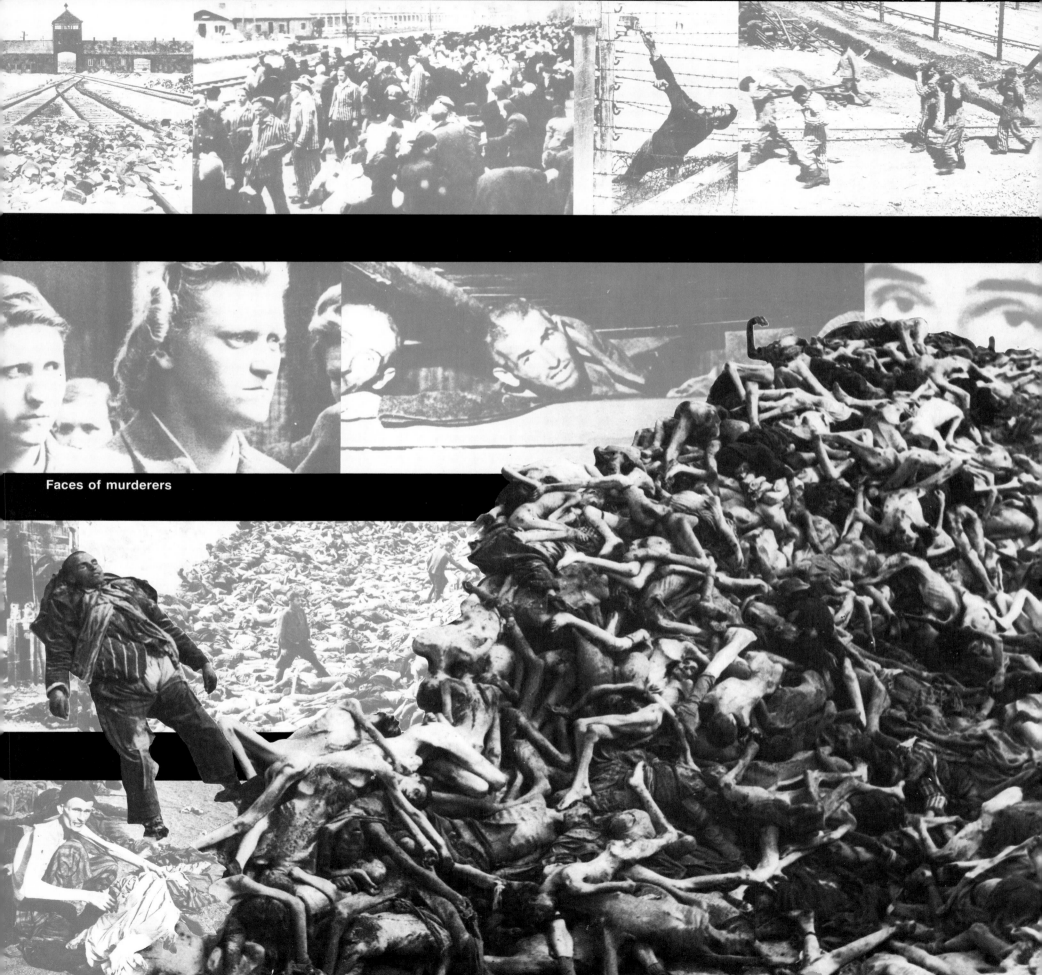

"Turn your eyes to the hill of corpses, students of history, pause for a moment and imagine that these poor remains, this bit of flesh and bone might be **your** father, **your** child, **your** wife, the person **you** loved."
(Eugen Kogon)

Faces of murderers

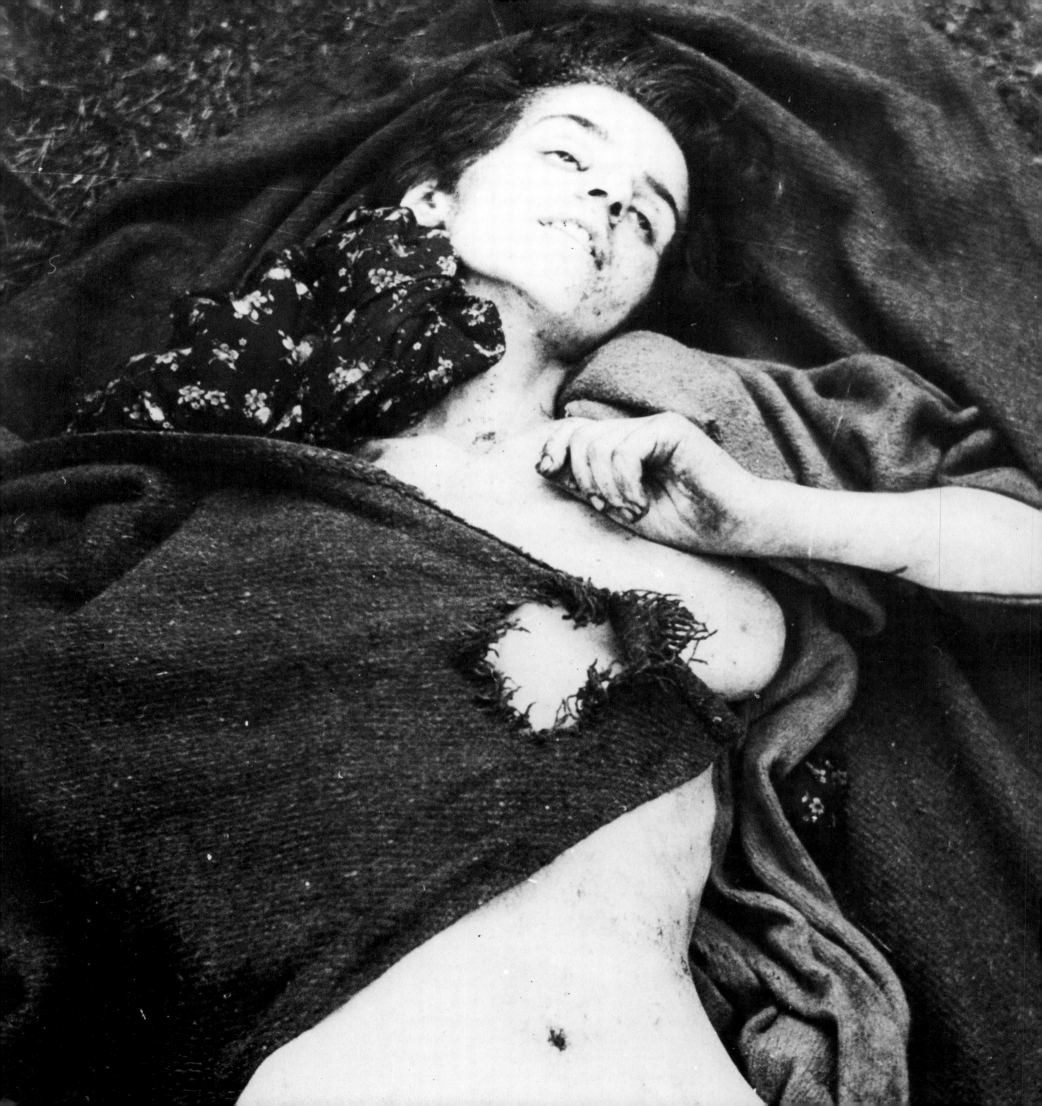

"The Truth, ...

...The Bitter Truth...."

(Danton, according to Stendhal)

We recognize today,
that many centuries of blindness
have veiled our eyes,
so that we no longer see the beauty of Your chosen people
and no longer recognize the features
of our first-born brother.
We know now that the mark of Cain is on our forehead
Over the course of centuries our brother Abel
has lain in the blood we have spilled,
and has wept tears which we have caused,
because we forgot Your love.
Forgive us for the curse,
which we unjustly placed on the name of the Jews.
Forgive us,
for crucifying You a second time.
For we knew not what we were doing....

Pope John XXIII
Prayer of Penance, written shortly before his death on June 3, 1963

Centres Of Jewish Life

Synagogues were not only places of worship but centres of Jewish communal life as well. Those built after the emancipation rivaled Christian churches in their impressive and monumental appearance. Among them were the synagogues in Posen (4) and Cottbus (10); and Berlin's Pestalozzistrasse (7), Rykestrasse (8), Prinzregentenstrasse (11), Heidereuther Gasse (12), and Fasanenstrasse (14, 15, 16). Some, like those on Kleine Auguststrasse (9) in Berlin, or in Stettin (13), stood among other structures in a row of buildings.

The synagogue Oranienburgerstrasse (1, 2, 3) in Berlin was the most imposing Jewish structure of the 19th century.

The introduction of organs in some synagogues (5: Lindenstrasse and 17, 18: Johannisstrasse, Berlin; 6: Stargard , Pomerania) was indicative of a trend within the Jewish reform movement to bring religious service closer to that of the gentile community.

The Jewish Holy Days

The Tora, the Five Books of Moses, prescribes six Holy Days and festivals: Shabbat, Rosh Hashana, Yom Hakippurim (Holy Days); and Pesah, Shavu'ot, and Sukkot (festivals). On those festivals in biblical times it was a religious duty to make a pilgrimage to the Temple in Jerusalem. Each of these Pilgrimage Festivals has a dual meaning: recalling the history of the people of Israel, and giving thanks for the new harvest, a symbol of ties to earth and to nature.

There are also other festivals, not prescribed in the Tora: Rosh Hodesh, Hanukka, Tu Be'Shvat, Purim, and Tish'a Be'Av.

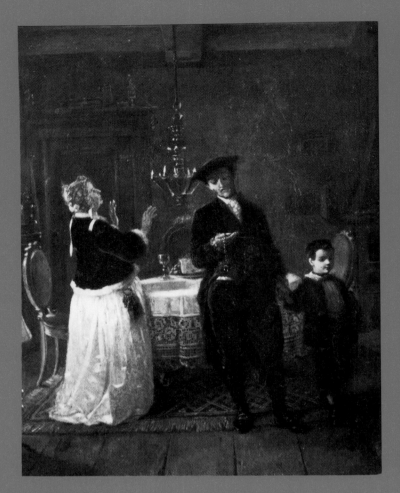

Beginning of the Shabbat

Blessing by the rabbi on Shabbat-morning

Shabbat, the day of rest

Shabbat (Sabbath)

Shabbat begins on Friday evening at sundown. On Shabbat eve the woman of the house lights two candles: Sahor, meaning Remember (II, 20:8); and Shamor, meaning Preserve (V, 5:12), a reference to the two passages in the Tora which command the observance of the Shabbat.

The Shabbat table is set with wine and bread — usually two loaves of bread to recall the double ration of manna gathered in the desert on the day before the Shabbat.

Shabbat is a day of rest after completion of the week's work (I, 2:1-3 "...and He rested on the seventh day....") The concept of a day of complete rest once a week originated with the Jews but has influenced the entire world.

Rosh Hodesh
(Festival of the New Moon)

Rosh Hodesh marks the beginning of the month according to the Jewish calendar. In the years before the Babylonian exile, no work was done on that day. Later its significance was limited to establishing the dates of Holy Days.

The new moon was ceremoniously hailed in Jerusalem; the news was then carried throughout the country by beacons lit on the top of mountains and by messengers. The delay in transmitting the news about the new moon's appearance was corrected by extending the duration of biblical feasts — with the exception of Yom Hakippurim — by one day for all Jews who lived at some distance from Jerusalem. This tradition persists to this day for Jews not living in Israel.

The ancient and solemn proclamation, "The new moon is hallowed," is still made during the announcement of the arrival of the new moon on the preceding Shabbat to seek God's blessing for the coming month.

The end of Shabbat

Feast of Tabernacles

Rosh Hashana (New Year) — the 1st of Tishri (Sept/Oct)

The beginning of the Jewish year and the start of the Ten Days of Atonement are the focus of Jewish religious life. On that day, considered the day of creation, God remembers all that He created. The sounding of the Shofar, a ram's horn, summons all believers to serious self-examination and atonement. The blowing of the Shofar has many meanings based on deeply religious motifs. It is a reminder of God's revelation on Mount Sinai (II, 19:16), proclaims the redemption of the people of Israel (Isaia 27:13), and recalls Abraham's willingness to sacrifice his own son.

Yom Hakippurim
(Yom Kippur = Day of Atonement) — the 10th of Tishri (Sept/Oct)

Yom Hakippurim, the last of the Ten Days of Atonement, is the holiest day in the Jewish religious year. It is a day of silence and humility. The texts read are Isaiah 57:14—58:14, in which unselfish love of one's neighbour is equated with true fasting, and the Book of Jonah, in which God's grace and atonement are also shown to heathens.

"He who says: I shall sin, and the Day of Atonement will bring me forgiveness, will not be granted atonement. Sins of man against God will be wiped out on the Day of Atonement; but sins against one's fellow man are forgiven only if the sinner and his victim have already been reconciled." (Talmud)

The wearing of a white garment is a sign of trust by the people of Israel in God. White, the colour worn for burial, is also a symbol of contrition and the frailty of man.

On the eve of the Day of Atonement

Sukkot (Feast of Tabernacles) — the 15th of Tishri (Sept/Oct)

Sukkot recalls the time when Jews lived in temporary dwellings in the deserts after the exodus from Egypt. It is also a harvest festival. During Sukkot, religious Jews are expected to dwell in or at least to eat their meals in the Sukka, a hut-like structure made from branches and boughs and decorated with fruits. On the seventh day, Hosha'na Rabba or Feast of Palms, worshippers wind their way through the synagogue seven times, carrying a bouquet of "the four species" (III, 23:40) in procession. The bouquet represents hope, harmony and a spirit of reconciliation. It consists of:

1. Citrus fruit (Etrog)
2. Palm branch (Lulav)
3. Three branches of myrtle (Hadasa)
4. Two willow branches (Arava)

Simhat Tora (Rejoicing in the Tora) designates the end of Sukkot; the Tora scrolls are carried through the synagogue in a festive procession, with children participating. Simhat Tora marks the completion of the synagogue reading of the Five Books of Moses, apportioned over the entire year. On this day, after the last section of the Fifth Book is read, the first verses of the First Book are recited. The words: "...He who makes the rain fall and the wind blow" are spoken for the first time as a special prayer for Israel, where the rainy season occurs during the winter months between Sukkot and Pesah.

The days between the festive beginning and the end of Sukkot are not full holidays.

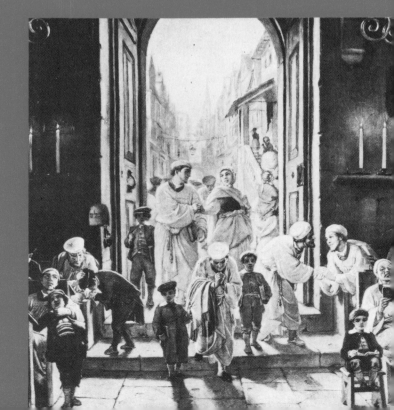

Hanukka —
the 25th of Kislev (Nov/Dec)

The Hanukka celebration commemorates the liberation and rededication of the Temple in 165 B.C.E., after he had been desecrated by Syrian-Greek heathens during the rule of the Seleucids. It recalls the victories of the Maccabees (167-165 B.C.E.) who broke their domination, gaining religious freedom and national independence for the Jewish people (the corresponding Tora portion is IV, 7:1 to 8:4).

The festival lasts eight days; it is linked to the miracle which occured when one day's supply of oil found in the Temple burned for eight days. On each day of Hanukka, an additional candle is lit after sundown. While the candles are burning, no work is permitted.

Tu Be'Shvat —
the 15th of Shvat (January/February)

Tu Be'Shvat celebrates the beginning of spring. One day each year in biblical times Jews payed a tithe in the form of fruits from trees to the Temple. Over the centuries that day was determined to be the 15th of Shvat, a time of the year when the trees still absorb rain and gain strength for the fall harvest. It is customary to celebrate the day by enjoying the fruits from fifteen varieties of trees. Today, in Israel, the 15th of Shvat is a day of tree planting.

Purim

Hanukk

Purim —
the 14th day of Adar (February/March)

The observance of Purim began in 40 B.C.E. and is the only festival which d not originate in Israel.

It is a reminder of the rescue of the Jewish people from great danger, as described in the Book of Esther. In ar hour of extreme peril for the Jews of Persia, Esther, the wife of the Persian King Ahasuerus, revealed her Jewish identity: "I and my people." Her confession saved the Jews, who were subject to the whims and will of the monarch.

Esther became a symbol for trust in th indestructibility of the Jewish people, example of the fate of Jews in the diaspora.

Purim is a happy celebration: children dress up, there is dancing and singing and presents are exchanged.

Pesah (Passover) —
the 15th of Nisan (March/April)

Pesah, which recalls the "passing over" of the homes of the Israelites (II. 12:12-13), marks the anniversary of the Exodus and is also a harvest festival (cutting of the barley).

The family celebration on the eve of the holiday is called Seder, the Hebrew term for "order," implying the specified order of the Passover ritual as set down in the Haggada, the book read on Passover which tells the story of the liberation of the people of Israel from Egyptian bondage.

The actual evolution of the Seder into a major religious family festivity began after the destruction of the Second Temple in 70 C.E.

The holiday table is set with two candles, wine, the Seder plate, and a cloth case with unleavened bread (Matsot). Each of these items has a special symbolism:

Three Matsot: the unleavened bread of affliction, serve as a reminder of the great haste in which the people of Israel fled Egypt

Zero'a: a roasted shankbone with bits of meat left on it, commemorates the sacrifice of the paschal lamb in the Temple

Betsa: one hard-boiled roasted egg recalls the offering in the Temple

Maror: bitter herbs, are a reminder of the bitterness of hard labour in Egyptian bondage

Haroset: a mixture of apples, nuts, cinnamon, and wine which symbolizes the clay and straw mixture with which the Jews were forced to make bricks for the Pharaoh's buildings

Karpas: parsley, radishes, celery or potatoes call to mind the meagre diet of slavery

Saltwater symbolizes the tears shed while in Egyptian bondage

A separate glass of wine is put on the table for the prophet Elias, whose presence at the Seder feast is eagerly awaited. Elias is the most popular prophet and mystic figure of the Jewish people. Post-biblical Judaism views him as a comforter of the poor and messenger of the Messiah.

The days between the festive beginning and the end of Pesah are not full holidays.

The period between Pesah and Shavu'ot is considered a time of mourning. These weeks gained additional significance as remembrance of the pogroms initiated by the Crusaders in 1096 and 1146.

The eve of Seder

There is only one day on which all rules of mourning, such as the prohibition of weddings, are suspended: Lag Ba'Omer.

Lag Ba'Omer
(Lag = the numerical value of 33)

It falls on Iyar 18, the 33rd day after Pesah. The celebration's origin dates back to the lifetime of Rabbi Akiva (50-135 C.E.) when an epidemic killed many of his students. On the 33rd day, Lag Ba'Omer, the terrible epidemic stopped.

Shavu'ot (Feast of the Weeks)

Shavu'ot, the only holyday with no fixed date in the Tora, falls seven weeks after the first day of Pesah. The count therefore begins on the 16th of Nisan (III. 23:15-16).

Shavu'ot commemorates the giving of the Law at Sinai and is a festival of the wheat harvest and the first fruits. During biblical times, two loaves of wheat bread would be brought to the Temple. While Pesah marks the beginning of the harvest with the cutting of the barley, Shavu'ot marks the final wheat harvest and is therefore also called the Concluding Festival.

The Book of Ruth, read on Shavu'ot, describes scenes from agricultural life and relates how Ruth, a heathen woman, converted to Judaism.

Tish'a Be'av —
the 19th of Av (July/August)

This is a day of mourning and fasting because on that day both Temples were destroyed — the First in 586 B.C.E., the Second in 70 C.E.. Songs of lamentation are read from the books of Job and Jeremiah. Many lamentations were added during later centuries in times of renewed distress.

Shavu'ot

Family Festivities

Brit Mila (Circumcision)

Circumcision takes place on the eighth day after the birth of a male child. At that time, the child is given his name. Circumcision is based on God's covenant with Abraham (I, 17:10-14): "...and you shall be circumcised in the flesh of your foreskin, and it shall be a token of a covenant between Me and you...."

Bar Mitsva

Bar Mitsva literally means "Son of Duty" and marks the initiation of a boy into adulthood in the eyes of religious law. On the Shabbat following his thirteenth birthday, the youngster is called up for the first time to read a portion of the Tora in the synagogue. Bar Mitsva is usually preceded by special instruction in the importance of the day and the meaning of the Shabbat. The youngster learns about his new religious duties and responsibilities and is taught how to put on the Talit (prayer shawl) and lay Tefilin (phylacteries).

Hatuna (Wedding)

When possible, a Jewish wedding in Western Europe takes place on Tuesday because that day is mentioned twice in the First Book: "God saw that it was good" (I, 1:10 and 12).

Both mothers, or girl friends of the bride, lead her to the Huppa (bridal canopy); the groom is led to the canopy by both fathers or by his friends. After two blessings, the couple drinks from a goblet of wine and the marriage ceremony begins. The groom places the ring on the bride's index finger and says: "With this ring may you be sanctified unto me according to the law of Moses and Israel." Then the marriage contract (Ketuba), which establishes the woman's rights, is read. Seven blessings mark the end of the ceremony; then the bride and groom again drink from the goblet of wine.

1 Brit Mila (Circumcision)
2 Bar Mitsva recital
3 The courtship
4 Hatuna (Wedding)

List Of Names

Abel, Alfred (1886-1937)
Abraham, Hermann (1847-1932)
Ahlwardt, Hermann (1846-1914)
Alsberg, Max (1877-1933)
Apt, Max (1869-1957)
Arnim, Bettina von (1785-1859)
Arons, Leo (1860-1919)
Arons, Levin (1773-1840)
Ascher, Saul (1767-1822)
Aschheim, Selmar (1878-1965)
Atlasz, Robert (born 1898)
Augustine, Aurelius St. (354-430)

Bab, Julius (1880-1955)
Baeck, Leo (1873-1956)
Bamberger, Ludwig (1823-1899)
Bandmann, Eugen (1874-1948)
Barnay, Ludwig (1842-1924)
Bebel, August (1840-1913)
Bendix, Alice (1895-1943)
Benjamin, Walter (1892-1940)
Ben Zion, Mossinson (1878-1942)
Bergner, Elisabeth (born 1897)
Berliner, Cora (1890-1942)
Berliner, Emil (1851-1929)
Bernhard, Georg (1875-1944)
Bernstein, Eduard (1850-1932)
Bernstorff, Christian Guenther
   (1769-1835)
Birnbaum, Nathan (1864-1937)
Bismarck, Otto von (1815-1898)
Blech, Leo (1871-1958)
Bleichroeder, Gerson (1822-1893)
Bloch, Iwan (1872-1922)
Blumenfeld, Kurt (1884-1963)
Bock, Hugo (1848-1932)
Bodenheimer, Max (1865-1940)
Born, Max (1882-1970)
Brahm, Otto (1856-1912)
Brandes, Simon Wolff
   (1688 and 1700 traceable)
Braun, Adolf (1862-1929)
Braun-Vogelstein, Julie (1883-1971)
Brentano, Clemens (1778-1842)
Buber, Martin (1878-1965)
Budko, Joseph (1888-1940)
Burg, Meno (1787-1853)

Callmann, Rudolph (1892-1976)
Chamisso, Adelbert von (1781-1838)
Clausewitz, Karl von (1780-1831)
Cohen, Hermann (1842-1918)
Cohn, Ferdinand Julius (1828-1898)
Crispien, Arthur (1875-1946)

Deutsch, Ernst (1890-1969)
Deutsch, Felix (1858-1928)
Doeblin, Alfred (1878-1957)
Dohm, Christian Wilhelm (1751-1820)
Droysen, Johann Gustav (1808-1884)
Duehring, Eugen (1833-1921)

Edison, Thomas Alva (1847-1931)
Ehrlich, Paul (1854-1915)
Eichhorn, Karl Friedrich von
   (1781-1854)
Einstein, Albert (1879-1955)
Eisenmenger, Johann Andreas
   (1654-1704)
Elbogen, Ismar (1874-1943)
Elsas, Fritz (1890-1945)
Engels, Friedrich (1820-1895)
Ephraim, Veitel Heine (1703-1775)

Falk, Bernhard (1867-1944)
Falkenstein, Julius (1880-1934)
Feiwel, Berthold (1875-1937)
Fichte, Johann Gottlieb (1762-1814)
Finkelstein, Heinrich (1865-1942)
Flatow, Alfred (1869-1942)
Fouqué, Friedrich Heinrich Karl
   de la Motte (1777-1843)

Fraenkel, Bernhard (1836-1911)
Franck, James (1882-1964)
Frankel, Zacharias (1801-1875)
Frankenthal, Kaethe (1889-1976)
Frankl, Wilhelm (1893- ?)
Frederick I, Elector (1372-1440)
Frederick I, King (1657-1713)
Frederick II, Elector (1413-1471)
Frederick II, King (1712-1786)
Frederick William, the Great Elector
   (1620-1688)
Frederick William I (1688-1740)
Frederick William II (1744-1797)
Frederick William III (1770-1840)
Frederick William IV (1795-1861)
Frey, Erich Max (1882-1964)
Friedlaender, David (1750-1834)
Friedemann, Adolf (1871-1932)
Fuerstenberg, Carl (1850-1933)

Gans, Eduard (1798-1839)
Gans, Leo (1843-1935)
Geiger, Abraham (1810-1874)
Gentz, Friedrich von (1764-1832)
Gerron, Kurt (1872-1944)
Goldstein, Moritz (1880-1977)
Graetz, Paul (1890-1938)
Granach, Alexander (1890-1949)
Gruenbaum, Fritz (1880-1940)
Gugenheim, Fromet
   → Mendelssohn, Fromet
Gundolf, Friedrich (1880-1931)

Haase, Hugo (1863-1919)
Hansen, Max (1900-1960)
Hantke, Arthur (1874-1955)
Harden, Maximilian (1861-1927)
Hardenberg, Karl August (1750-1822)
Hegel, Georg Wilhelm Friedrich
   (1770-1831)
Heilmann, Ernst (1881-1940)
Heine, Heinrich (1797-1856)
Hermann, Georg (1871-1943)
Herxheimer, Karl (1861-1942)
Herz, Henriette (1764-1847)
Herzl, Theodor (1860-1904)
Hess, Moses (1812-1875)
Hess, Willy (1859-1939)
Hirsch, Otto (1885-1941)
Hirsch, Paul (1868-1940)
Hirsch, Rahel (1870-1953)
Hirsch, Samson Raphael
   (1808-1888)
Hirschfeld, Magnus (1868-1935)
Hitzig, Friedrich (1811-1881)
Hollaender, Felix (1867-1931)
Hollaender, Friedrich (1896-1976)
Hollaender, Victor (1866-1940)
Horkheimer, Max (1895-1973)
Huenefeld, Guenther von (1892-1929)
Humboldt, Alexander von (1769-1859)
Humboldt, Wilhelm von (1767-1835)

Innocent III. (1143-1216)
Israel, James (1848-1926)
Itzig, Isaac Daniel (1750-1806)

Jacob, Martel (1910-1976)
Jacobsohn, Egon (1895-1969)
Jacobson, Victor (1869-1934)
Jacoby, Johann (1805-1877)
Jahn, Friedrich Ludwig (1778-1852)
Jastrow, Ignaz (1856-1937)
Jean Paul (1763-1825)
Jessner, Leopold (1878-1945)
Joachim I Nestor, Elector (1484-1535)
Joachim II, Elector (1505-1571)
Joachim, Joseph (1831-1907)
Josel of Rosheim (1480-1554)
Jungmann, Max (1875-1970)

Kalisch, David (1820-1872)
Kant, Immanuel (1724-1804)
Karminski, Hannah (1897-1942)
Kauffmann, Meyer (1779-1851)
Kempner, Friederike (1838-1904)
Kempner, Maximilian (1854-1927)
Kerr, Alfred (1867-1948)
Klee, Alfred (1875-1943)
Kleist, Heinrich von (1777-1811)
Klemperer, Otto (1885-1973)
Klewitz, Anton Wilhelm von (1760-1838)
Kortner, Fritz (1892-1970)
Kristeller, Samuel (1820-1900)
Kronecker, Leopold (1823-1891)
Kunstmann, Wilhelm (1844-1934)

Laband, Paul (1838-1918)
Lang, Fritz (1890-1976)
Lasker, Eduard (1829-1884)
Lasker-Schueler, Else (1869-1945)
Lassalle, Ferdinand (1825-1864)
Lavater, Johann Kaspar (1741-1801)
Lazarus, Moritz (1824-1903)
Ledebour, Georg (1850-1947)
Lessing, Gotthold Ephraim (1729-1781)
Lessing, Theodor (1872-1933)
Levin, Markus (1723-1790)
Levin, Shmarya (1867-1935)
Levin-Varnhagen von Ense, Rahel
   (1771-1833)
Lewald, Fanny (1811-1889)
Lewald, Theodor (1860-1947)
Lichtheim, Richard (1885-1963)
Liebermann, Max (1847-1935)
Liebknecht, Karl (1871-1919)
Lilien, Ephraim Moshe (1874-1925)
Lindenau, Heinrich (1872-1942)
Lippold (about 1520-1573)
Loewe, Heinrich (1869-1951)
Loewen, Sara (1769-1839)
Loewenfeld, William (1851-1931)
Lobethal, Esther (1753-1827)
Lobethal, Victor Aaron (1744-1813)
Louis Ferdinand Prince of Prussia
   (1772-1806)
Lucca, Pauline (1841-1908)
Ludwig, Margrave (1315-1361)
Luria, Joseph (1871-1937)
Luther, Martin (1483-1546)
Luxemburg, Rosa (1871-1919)

Maassen, Karl Georg von (1760-1834)
Magnus, Heinrich Gustav (1802-1870)
Magnus, Julius (1867-1944)
Maimon, Salomon (1754-1800)
Mannheim, Lucie (1899-1976)
Marwitz, Friedrich August Ludwig
   (1777-1837)
Marx, Karl (1818-1883)
Massary, Fritzi (1882-1969)
Mayer, Helene (1910-1953)
Mehring, Walter (1896-1981)
Meitner, Lise (1878-1968)
Mendelsohn, Erich (1887-1953)
Mendelssohn, Abraham (1776-1835)
Mendelssohn, Eleonore von (1900-1951)
Mendelssohn, Fromet (1725-1812)
Mendelssohn, Joseph (1770-1848)
Mendelssohn, Moses (1729-1786)
Mendelssohn Bartholdy, Ernst von
   (1846-1909)
Mendelssohn Bartholdy, Fanny
   (1805-1847)
Mendelssohn Bartholdy, Felix
   (1809-1847)
Mendelssohn Bartholdy, Lea
   (1777-1842)
Metternich, Klemens Fürst von
   (1773-1859)
Meyer, Franz (1897-1972)
Mirabeau, Honoré Gabriel (1749-1791)
Mommsen, Theodor (1817-1903)
Morgenstern, Lina (1830-1909)
Moser, Moses (1796-1838)
Moses, Julius (1868-1942)
Moses, Siegfried (1887-1974)
Mosheim, Grete (born 1905)
Mosse, Marcus (1808-1865)
Mosse, Rudolf (1843-1920)
Motz, Friedrich von (1775-1830)
Motzkin, Leo (1867-1933)
Mueller, Adam Heinrich (1779-1829)

Napoleon I (1769-1821)
Neher, Carola (1905-1940)
Nelson, Rudolf (1878-1960)
Nicolai, Christoph Friedrich (1733-1811)
Nordau, Max (1849-1923)

Ochs, Siegfried (1858-1929)
Oppenheim, Moritz Daniel (1799-1882)
Oppenheimer, Franz (1864-1943)
Orlik, Emil (1870-1932)

Pallenberg, Max (1877-1934)
Pappenheim, Bertha (1859-1936)
Preuss, Hugo (1860-1925)
Pueckler-Muskau, Hermann Prince of
   (1785-1871)

Ranke, Leopold von (1795-1886)
Rathenau, Emil (1838-1915)
Rathenau, Walther (1867-1922)
Reinhardt, Max (1873-1943)
Rosenblueth, Felix (1887-1978)
Ruehs, Christian Friedrich (1779-1820)

Sachs, Michael (1808-1864)
Sachs, Nelly (1891-1970)
Salomon, Alice (1872-1948)
Diss: as 85 / File: register-1
Salomon, Erich (1886-1944)
Savigny, Friedrich Karl von (1779-1861)
Schadow, Johann Gottfried (1764-1850)
Schauer, Rudolf (1869-1930)
Schlegel, Dorothea (1772-1839)
Schleiermacher, Friedrich Ernst Daniel
   (1768-1834)
Schlenther, Paul (1854-1916)
Schlesinger, Georg (1874-1949)
Schlesinger, Paul (1878-1928)
Seligsohn, Julius L. (1890-1942)
Senator, Hermann (1834-1911)
Simon, Ernst Emanuel (born 1898)
Simon, James (1851-1932)
Simson, Eduard von (1810-1899)
Simson, Hermann (1897-1967)
Singer, Paul (1844-1911)
Sophie Charlotte (1668-1705)
Stahl, Heinrich (1868-1942)
Stein, Karl Freiherr vom (1757-1831)
Steinheim, Salomon Ludwig (1789-1866)
Steinthal, Heymann (1823-1899)
Stoecker, Adolf (1835-1909)
Struck, Hermann (1876-1944)
Syrkin, Nachman (1867-1924)

Tieck, Ludwig (1773-1853)
Tietz, Hermann (1837-1907)
Tischler, Heinrich (1892-1938)
Treitschke, Heinrich von (1834-1896)
Trietsch, Davis (1870-1935)
Trotzky, Leon (1879-1940)
Tucholsky, Kurt (1890-1935)

Ullstein, Franz (1868-1945)
Ullstein, Hans (1859-1935)
Ullstein, Hermann (1875-1943)
Ullstein, Leopold (1826-1899)
Ullstein, Louis Ferdinand (1863-1933)
Ullstein, Rudolf (1873-1964)
Ury, Lesser (1861-1931)
Ussishkin, Menachem Mendel (1863-1941)

Valentin, Martin (1779-1851)
Valetti, Rosa (1878-1937)
Vallentin, Hermann (1872-1938)
Varnhagen von Ense, Karl August
   (1785-1858)
Varnhagen von Ense, Rahel
   → Levin-Varnhagen
Veidt, Conrad (1893-1943)
Veit, Moritz (1808-1864)
Virchow, Rudolf (1821-1902)

Walden, Herwarth (1878-1943)
Waldenburg, Ludwig (1837-1881)
Wallburg, Otto (1893-1941)
Walter, Bruno (1876-1962)
Warburg, Emil (1846-1931)
Warschauer, Malvin (1871-1955)
Weiss, Bernhard (1880-1951)
Weissgerber, Andreas (1901-1942)
Weizmann, Chajim (1874-1952)
Weltsch, Robert (1891-1982)

Werbezirk, Gisela (1875-1956)
Wertheimer, Josef, Edler Ritter von
   (1800-1887)
William I (1797-1888)
William II (1859-1941)
Wittgenstein, Ludwig Adolf Peter
   (1769-1843)
Wolff, Bernhard (1811-1879)
Wolff, Leo (1870-1958)
Wolff, Theodor (1868-1943)
Wolffsohn, David (1856-1914)

Zetkin, Clara (1857-1933)
Zunz, Leopold (1794-1886)
Zweig, Arnold (1887-1968)

Bibliographical Sources

Numerous studies have been published on various
aspects of the history of German Jewry. It would be
beyond our capacity to enumerate all of these
works. For those interested in further information,
we recommend the *Leo Baeck Institute Year Book,*
published for the Leo Baeck Institute by Secker &
Warburg, London, and the *Jahrbuch des Instituts
fuer Deutsche Geschichte,* University of Tel Aviv,
edited by Walter Grab. These year books contain
relevant essays and a wealth of bibliographical sources.

Picture Credits

AEG Firmenarchiv, Brunswick
Amerika-Gedenkbibliothek, Berlin
Berlin Museum, Berlin
Beth Hatefutsoth (Walter Gierke), Tel Aviv
Bildarchiv Preussischer Kulturbesitz, Berlin
Bildstelle Hanau
Black Star, New York
Bote & Bock, Berlin
Werner Braun, Jerusalem
Central Zionist Archives, Jerusalem
Geheimes Staatsarchiv
  Preussischer Kulturbesitz, Berlin
Thomas Goldstein, New York
Mrs. Oscar and Mr. Emanuel Grusz, New York
Catherine Hanf-Noren, New York
Israel Museum, Jerusalem
Juedische Gemeinde zu Berlin
Jewish Museum, New York
Landesbildstelle Berlin
Leo Baeck Institute, New York
Ernst G. Lowenthal, Berlin
Maccabi World Union, Tel Aviv
Mendelssohn-Archiv Statsbibliothek
  Preussischer Kulturbesitz, Berlin
Nationalgalerie
  Preussischer Kulturbesitz, Berlin
Kurt Nemitz, Bremen
Abraham Pisarek, Berlin
David Rubinger, Jerusalem
Bagdikian Serkis, Berlin
Stadtarchiv Frankfurt am Main
Tel Aviv Museum, Tel Aviv
Ullstein-Bilderdienst, Berlin
US Air Force, Dept. of Defense,
  Washington, DC
Yad Vashem, Jerusalem
Walter Zadek, Tel Aviv

All the pictures of the Jewish festivities were taken
from the cyclus "Jüdisches Familienleben" by Moritz
Daniel Oppenheim (1799-1882). The photographs
of the original paintings are presented here for the
first time with the kind permission of Mr. Oscar and
Mr. Emanuel Gruss, New York.

ISBN 3-88053-017-3